A WRITER'S JOURNAL WORKBOOK

Creating space for writers to be inspired

Lucy van Smit

BLOOMSBURY YEARBOOKS
LONDON · OXFORD · NEW YORK · NEW DELHI · SYDNEY

BLOOMSBURY YEARBOOKS
Bloomsbury Publishing Plc
50 Bedford Square, London, WC1B 3DP, UK
29 Earlsfort Terrace, Dublin 2, Ireland

BLOOMSBURY, BLOOMSBURY YEARBOOKS, WRITERS' & ARTISTS' and the Diana logo
are trademarks of Bloomsbury Publishing Plc

First published in Great Britain 2022

A catalogue record for this book is available from the British Library

ISBN: PB: 978-1-4729-8736-5; eBook: 978-1-4729-8866-9

4 6 8 10 9 7 5 3

Typeset by Deanta Global Publishing Services, Chennai, India
Printed and bound in Great Britain by CPI Group (UK) Ltd, Croydon CR0 4YY

To find out more about our authors and books, visit www.bloomsbury.com
and sign up for our newsletters

CONTENTS

INTRODUCTION

Find out who you are and do it on purpose.

DOLLY PARTON

YOUR WRITING LIFE

You will change and grow many times in your writing life. This workbook aims to champion your journey. It answers those tricky questions you long to ask, shares practices to inspire your writing confidence and to free your unique gifts from common obstacles and writing worries. You'll discover surprising new techniques from acting, neuroscience, psychology, philosophy and spirituality to re-wild your creativity and empower your writing craft.

Writing can seem overwhelming. You long to be a writer, but where do you start? And how do you bridge the gap between where you are right now and where you want to go? How do you discover your voice? What does that even mean? And what can you do to improve your writing? Or discover what you want to write about?

You might read a book on writing craft, brave a writing class, feel inspired on the day, but at home, tiny doubts come at you again like mosquitoes. You get stung awake in the night with your worst fear: what if you're no good at this writing malarkey?

Good writing takes commitment and practice, but you also need passion and opportunity. Creating this space can be a challenge when society and schooling values exams and success over creativity and can leave you with little time to explore your inner world.

It takes courage to realise that you are a writer. And it's likely that you don't know exactly what kind of writer you are yet, or have found what you love to write about. No writer is born knowing these things, but one day you recognise the spark that can grow into your passion.

This book will help you to find that spark. You get to decide if it stays a reliable pilot light, or burns out of control. This is your writing life, write it your way.

Achieving excellence in any field is a continuous process. You are the expert on your own life, and only you can take that unique experience into your writing.

UNIVERSAL LAWS

There are no rules in life or in writing, but some things are true for everyone.

The same laws that govern nature and the universe, govern your soul, your head, your heart and mind – your creative power houses.

Writers often forget that these laws shape their writing practice. For example, apply the Law of Cause and Effect to writing a novel and you will discover the Universal Law of Creativity:

The Muse Shows Up When You Do.

But ignore the Law of Balance, and overwork with no rest, and the Muse will slip away, because you will be too distracted and exhausted to listen. These universal laws are based on human observation and experience.

And so is good writing. Your writing journal is a priceless resource; it helps you to see and feel more.

The universe is a work in progress. And so are you. You live in exciting, chaotic times. No one has more potential to navigate life and tell themselves a better story than a writer.

When a writer makes sense and meaning from life, we call it a story.

INSTINCTS

Trust your own instincts. What works for one writer might not be good for you.

Every writer is as unique as their fingertips, and if you've not found what to write about yet, a writing journal will connect you to your passion.

This yearning to write is your soul calling you to live a bigger creative life. Allow writing to be your teacher, follow where it leads and it will pull you along the path with enthusiasm, barking, *Look at this! Smell that! Over here!* Writing sees ordinary life as a brave new world. It digs up secrets you had no idea existed inside you.

Why journal? Because you don't learn from experience; you learn when you reflect on your experiences and this self-awareness brings your writing alive. You enter a deeper relationship with yourself. A sense of knowing. Ancient Greek philosophers valued self-reflection and now Harvard run a Journal Project to help its students stay mentally healthy – it found that students become 23% more productive and engaged with their studies when they journal.

In short, the writer who journals feels happier and writes better.

A writing journal gives you agency over your writing. It holds your feet to the fire of who you are. Creativity needs you to let go of the cultural obsession with mastery and control. Set your writing free. Play. Give yourself space, permission to explore your own nature with curiosity and a sense of adventure. Above all, explore who you are as a writer, with kindness, with wonder.

Don't rush ahead of yourself and worry about how to get published. Instead, focus on being in the moment when you write. Shift from seeking the external approval of others, to gaining a deep-down sense of your own identity and inner purpose.

Why listen to me? I am a writer and an artist. My signature strength is curiosity, a love of learning. I have read and talked to hundreds of writers and experts over thirty-five years. I am a creative person who knows success and failure and how to manage anxiety.

I started out as a painter, switched to television and made multiple arts documentaries on authors, from John Le Carré and P. D. James to Ian McEwan. I interview writers at the London Screenwriters' Festival but I became an award-winning author only when, like you, I finally listened to the voice that whispered, 'you're a writer too'. It took me decades to pay attention to it, and I made every mistake going along the way. I hope to speed things up for you.

I know the joy of sitting down and writing a whole novel from start to finish in one go. And I know how dreadful it feels to be stuck and stumble headlong into writer's block. I dug my way out, but I made it hard – when it could have been so easy – because I didn't slow down to listen.

My passion is to inspire you to write well without the anxiety. I wish I'd known what I am about to share with you. This is not a book about getting published or finding an agent. This is a book about finding *you*. Finding your voice. Trusting your talent. Your creativity. It is about putting your heart and soul into your writing practice.

Do the prompts and exercises. Reflect. By the end of the book, you will find a sense of feeling grounded in your own writing. A Knowing. When you pay close attention to your life and unleash your intention to write, insights, ideas, synchronicities, writing confidence and word-skills rush in. They change you into a happy, productive writer. And this book will prompt you to practise, practise, practise, until your writing becomes a joyful habit in your busy life.

ACT ONE

PRACTICE

SURPRISING SOLUTIONS
TO TRICKY PROBLEMS

YOUR SECRET ADVANTAGE

Isn't it splendid to think of all the things there are to find out
about? It just makes me feel glad to be alive ...

LUCY MAUD MONTGOMERY

A BEGINNER'S MIND

The surprising secret advantage for an emerging writer is your 'beginner's mind'. Think of this not as being childish, but childlike. Unselfconscious. Imaginative. Courageous. Playful. Geniuses from Einstein to Picasso spent their lives trying see the world as a child again. What if you never lost your beginner's mind? And you cherished a childlike curiosity in your writing from the start?

Childlike is fun, an easy way to be fully in the moment, just watch how a small child explores a sandpit or plays make believe. Playing games develops our most sophisticated kind of thinking, what scientists call counterfactual reasoning, which is your ability to imagine complex hypothetical scenarios and their consequences. It's what you do when you write a story.

AWE IS IN THE MOMENT

Being childlike is your golden ticket into creativity. Don't lose your way by following the herd. Take your time to wonder about things that others forget to look at with awe. Discover your preferences. Your own preoccupations. Your own mistakes. Resist the temptation to run ahead of yourself and worry if your writing is good enough to get published. Like a footballer out to win the championship, you must keep your focus on the immediate next step, or you will get anxious and tighten up. Stay in the moment.

HOW DO YOU GET GOING?

The secret of getting ahead is getting started. The secret of getting started is breaking your complex overwhelming tasks into small manageable tasks, and then starting on the first one.

MARK TWAIN

Every journey starts from where you happen to be at the time and writing is no exception. You start exactly where you are. Start right now. Grab a pen and get ready to write.

Feel a bit overwhelmed? Don't worry. Your passion for writing, and a sense of being dazed, are what bring most writers to their first writing class: excitement – the feeling that you are in the right place – and confusion – when conflicting versions of you seem to pop up and battle it out inside, each one shouting instructions or telling you to go the other way.

Doubts are natural. And the most talented writers often have the most doubts; they have a harder time recognising their unique gifts. The surprising knack to writing confidence is to let go. Relax.

At any stage, your writing can get snarled up, just as wet bedsheets get tangled up in the wash. It can be hard to see where one thing ends and another begins, and you might struggle to sort everything out. But when you relax and allow yourself to enjoy the process, it's also where the fun lies. Start with the nearest bit to you. Observe yourself, and gently unravel what you've got.

If you wrestle, pull too hard, too impatiently, you get tied up in knots. Give up too soon, things dry up stiff and creased, and a muddle won't look or feel as beautiful on the page, or on your bed. The trick is to treat everything, even wet bedsheets, but especially your writing, with compassion and respect. Tackle things bit by bit, so you feel encouraged by your progress and can work out your next move. It helps to play with some basic skills.

THE NAMING GAME

We are important and our lives are important, magnificent really, and their details are worthy to be recorded. This is how writers must think, this is how we must sit down with pen in hand. We were here: we are human beings: this is how we lived…

NATALIE GOLDBERG

The secret to a brilliant writing practice starts with NOTICING.

And NAMING the things around you.

It sounds so simple, but this daily practice tunes you like a radio station into your writing life. The Naming Game is a simple way to take the first step, it brings you into the moment.

Don't rush this step. It is astounding how grounded you become as a writer when you pay more attention to your ordinary world, and when you take a moment to notice how you respond to it.

How you feel about things and life events, what you notice about them, is what makes you a writer.

This skill develops quickly and becomes more nuanced over time. Walking down a familiar street fascinates you anew. You can feel yourself waking up, and you will effortlessly begin to notice more complex things. You wonder about the words people choose to use, and how they move through their lives. Example: you notice the man feeding pigeons so they poop on his neighbour's car and you wonder what happened in his life to make him so difficult. You seek to understand, not judge.

Practise this first step of The Naming Game and learn to switch between your ordinary and a writer's way of seeing. Picasso said when he ate a tomato, he just saw a tomato as a tomato. But when he looked at a tomato as an artist, he saw it as art. Rest your writer's eye often, and remember to enjoy walking down the street just being you.

WHERE ARE YOU?

I kept always two books in my pocket, one to read, one to write in.

ROBERT LOUIS STEVENSON

Where are you? In this exercise, I mean this quite literally. Which room are you in? Maybe you're reading in bed or in a café or the kitchen? LOOK UP: what do you see? Set a timer for seven minutes and write down what you see around you. Don't skip ahead; name and DESCRIBE things in your own words.

STARTER SENTENCE: I am looking at…

YOUR WRITING JOURNAL

Attention without feeling is only a report.

MARY OLIVER

What happens when you look up and simply write down what you see? Can you feel how The Naming Game grounds you? When I road-tested this practice, I found that naming things works like a meditation and pulls you into the present moment. But what do you think?

Did it take the pressure off you to write 'perfectly'? Did it help you to write in more detail? Take a moment to check in with yourself.

PROMPT: My feeling about this is…

Description now concentrates on setting and atmosphere, rather than telling us authoritatively how the hero or heroine feels.

BARRY CUNNINGHAM

Look up, again. Write about one small thing that stands out for you. A jug. A person. Set a timer for three minutes. What did the one small thing spark? A childhood memory? The way someone is standing?

STARTER SENTENCE: I noticed...

I'M STUCK. WHAT SHOULD I DO?

A writer is somebody for whom writing is more
difficult than it is for other people.

THOMAS MANN

TRY THIS: MAKE A LIST

In creative writing, describing a room, or a view, or even your cat, can feel very daunting. If you get stuck, or worry how to write a good sentence, start with an inventory, a list.

Name and list what you see around you, but write them down on the same line, as if they were in a sentence. In such a simple exercise, the magic starts to happen. A list wants to grow into sentences. Unbidden, you make connections between you as the writer and what you notice.

> EXAMPLE:
>
> The list of things next to me: the oak breadboard, lip-salve tin, mirrored coaster, snapdragons in vase, tarnished silver teaspoon, yellow box of cooking matches, basil leaves in jar of manky water, round mahogany table, badly warped. (Which is why my laptop is on the breadboard.) Kitchen scissors with orange handles, John O'Donohue's aqua-green book of poems, an empty porcelain fruit bowl, pale dawn light, old writing paper layered like filo pastry, my cold hands on the keyboard, red nail varnish, badly chipped.

A list of things saves you a lot of time and bother, it's one of the best kept writing secrets.

Have a go.

THE LIST GAME

Complexity is the enemy of execution.

TONY ROBBINS

Look up, and list what you see. Start with nouns; the name of things. Write your list on the page as if it were a sentence, with each item separated by a comma. Avoid resistance and your inner critic by doing it right now. Start close in. It is much easier to start with the nearest things to you, on your table or your bed or sofa. Set a timer for three minutes. The trick is to write with awe – imagine you are a stranger listing these things in their head for the first time, marvelling at this strange new world. Come back to the starter sentence whenever you get stuck and begin again.

STARTER SENTENCE: When I look up, I see…

WHY WORKSHOP YOURSELF?

Life is the biggest workshop: you have to observe life.

AYUSHMANN KHURRANA

———

Creative writing is often taught in the workshop format. Writers submit their work to be read and critiqued by a small tutorial group. A workshop is a practical way to teach writing by getting students to write regularly. You learn to give and receive feedback, face to face. A writing workshop needs to be a safe space for you to be able to make mistakes and keep writing.

Novelist George Saunders picks six of the 'best' writers from 700 applicants and workshops their writing, through a three-year Creative Writing Program. George Saunders says the students' writing was already wonderful. But what these writers don't know is WHO they are.

They may not know HOW they feel. WHY they love certain things. In short, they don't know what makes them, them. Your writing journal asks you the same questions.

———

WHAT MAKES YOU, YOU?

How do you feel about your writing? Why do you respond to it that way? It's not about right or wrong. It is about being you. When you show us who you are, you show us who we are.

———

A WRITER SHOWS US WHO WE ARE

And a writing journal is your secret weapon to do this. I wish I'd known this when I became a writer. This practice connects you to yourself like a conversation with an old friend: You show up. Share. Listen. Learn. You find out what you think, about what you just said, and how you really feel. This saves you years of beating yourself up and moving too fast in the wrong direction.

SELF-REFLECTION EMPOWERS...

Self-reflection is a powerful tool for your writing. It is the compassionate *intention* to know yourself and to understand how you respond to life. This self-awareness can inspire a high level of clarity that helps you to make better writing decisions and to avoid pitfalls.

...BUT RUMINATION KEEPS YOU STUCK

Rumination is when you go over and over the same thought in your head. Rumination stresses you out. Your mind and your body re-experience the event as if it were actually happening again.

This disempowering habit gobbles up brain space and leaves you with less energy to write. You feel like you are writing, because you are thinking about your writing, but you are stuck and not actually getting words down on the page. Treat rumination like another wet bedsheet – untangle the mess bit by bit. And get repetitive worries out of your head; dump them in your writing journal.

When you become aware of a bad habit, don't criticise yourself. Be curious. Awareness alone is enough to release unhelpful thoughts without the need for judgement. This workbook is your private workshop. You give and receive feedback. You hold yourself accountable to write more.

THE WORKSHOP GAME

Live each day as if your life had just begun.

GOETHE

Go back. Take a moment to reflect on The Naming Game exercise.

How did you respond to it? Could you describe the place where you are with ease? Did your writing unfold and itch to say more? Or did you worry how to get it right?

Did you get stuck in Analysis Paralysis? Overthinking? (Another of my many weak spots.)

Did your resistance show up and give you an excuse not to do it? Listen out for the trickster voice in your head that tells you something is too easy; don't bother. This is our fear disguised as an old friend. Stay in the arena, take action by writing.

Or did you find you knew exactly what you wanted to say? And smashed it? Set an intention to notice your strengths and praise yourself. Praise releases dopamine.

How do you feel about using a writing journal? Does it feel daunting or liberating? Like every new practice, start small. Enthusiasm without roots burns out fast.

WRITING PRACTICE

Your first writing tool is The Naming Game. Start today. Start small. Notice the things around you, jot down your observations. What have you missed that is under your nose? Do you know what trees you have in your street? Capture them in a notebook; record stuff on your phone as you walk. Chanting the name of things in your head trains your eye and gets you thinking as a writer. Keep asking yourself: What do I see? It's astonishing how quickly this simple trick trains your eyes and ears, and how alive the world around you seems when you are more present in it.

WRITE IT DOWN

WHAT you can say in your head and HOW you can get that down on paper are two different beasts. A writer spends a lifetime trying to bridge that gap. The Naming Game helps you to avoid your worst enemy – analysis paralysis. Just get anything down on paper and you can write more.

STOP. LOOK. WRITE.

Do this three times on a writing day. Then have a rest day. Neuroscience shows that your brain grows to adapt to a new skill when you rest. And you look forward to writing the next day, because you can see the improvement, rather than it become another thing you feel you *should* do.

Set a reminder on your phone. When a writing timer goes off, be like Pavlov's dogs: react instantly and write. A quick sketch trains your eye. Write down exactly what you see where you are at that moment. Don't judge whether it's a subject worth your time. Write in the pub, on a bus, in a queue for coffee, watching the kids not eat their lunch. Do it in your head if you are driving.

Ask yourself: what do you see?

_____

How does it make you feel?

_____

What are you touching? Can you feel the smooth handrail as you walk downstairs?

_____

Why is this such an important skill to develop? You make sense of the world via your perception.

It is the doorway into your writing. When you look up from your screen and name one thing at a time, you bring awareness to the everyday.

This naming practice helps you to be more present in your life. You start to think about writing as a bridge between you and the world, rather than a wall.

THE COUCH TO 5K GAME

Bring me the sunset in a cup.

EMILY DICKINSON

A regular habit takes you further than flashes of inspiration. If you are out of practice, try the 'Couch to 5k' approach. You will get your writing practice up and running in no time.

DAY ONE

Set an alarm to write for twenty minutes.

Set another timer for one minute on repeat.

Write for one minute; when the timer goes off, relax.

Stretch/breathe for one minute.

Repeat the one-minute pattern until the twenty minutes is up.

DAY TWO

This is a rest day. Instead of writing: Read for five minutes.

DAY THREE

Set an alarm to write for twenty minutes. Set another timer for two minutes at a time.

Write for two minutes. Then stretch/breathe for one minute.

Repeat this on/off pattern until your twenty minutes' writing time is up.

DAY FOUR

Rest. Read for ten minutes.

DAY FIVE

Write for three minutes.

Then break for a one-minute stretch/breathe.

Repeat for twenty minutes.

WEEKS TWO–SIX

Gradually increase writing sprints to five minutes, then eight minutes, then ten minutes. Keep the one-minute stretch/breathe time until you can concentrate and write in half-hour blocks. Build consistency. Not burn out. Read on your rest days: and steadily increase your reading time to thirty minutes. Once again, start small to build a life-long habit.

MORNING PRACTICE

On your Writing Day, in the mornings: STOP. LOOK. WRITE down what you see. Set a reminder. Keep the workbook with you and whip it out when the times goes off and write for two minutes. Name what you see. Try this waiting in the car, or for the family to get out the door.

I am looking at…

I am looking at…

I am looking at…

I am looking at…

I am looking at…

I am looking at…

I am looking at…

This reminds me of…

(EXAMPLE: the cereal box that unfolds a memory of student days.)

AFTERNOON PRACTICE

STOP. LOOK. WRITE down what you see. Try this while you eat a sandwich or are queuing. Set a reminder. When the timer goes off, look up. What do you see? Where are you?

I am looking at…

I am looking at…

I am looking at…

I am looking at…

I am looking at…

I am looking at…

I am looking at…

This reminds me of…

EVENING PRACTICE

STOP. LOOK. WRITE down what you see. Breathe in the spirit of wherever you are. No excuses. Set a reminder. Write for two minutes. The shock of the timer stops you being off somewhere in your head, and once again you are in the moment. What do you see? How does it make you feel?

I am looking at…

I am looking at…

I am looking at…

I am looking at…

I am looking at…

I am looking at…

I am looking at…

This reminds me of…

WHY START SMALL?

You can kick-start a whole book with some little writing exercise.

HILARY MANTEL

In *Writing Down the Bones*, Natalie Goldberg recommends you practise writing for two years before you attempt a novel. I didn't know this when I became a writer and I doubt I would have listened.

My first novel poured out of me – it was thrilling to write. And I signed up for a Creative Writing MA. The tutor said I would learn more if I started a new novel. So, I parked that first book. I began to write shorter pieces, experimenting with ideas for a scene, or a short story. A new novel grew out of that shorter-pieces practice, which won an award and got published. But it took me years and years to get to that level. I had to unlearn some very bad habits that I picked up with my first book, like over-complicating the plot and leaving no space for the characters to breathe.

Goldberg's advice to start small seems slow, but if you can master the art of writing down the 'bones' of what you see, think and feel, it will save you time and heartache in the long run.

A novel is a juggernaut. It is hard to manoeuvre when you make a mistake. Many writers get disheartened and lose their way. But when you look up and learn to write down what you see, you can nip around in a Mini, have start up adventures, and learn your craft. You will naturally move on to writing scenes, short stories, and then a book.

Start small, be gentle on yourself. And self-disciplined. Practise. Then writing becomes a habit.

(P.S. If you skipped the writing exercises, go back and do them.)

THE NEXT STEP

I think I may boast myself to be, with all possible vanity, the most unlearned and uninformed female who ever dared to be an authoress.

JANE AUSTEN

The Naming Game automatically moves your mind onto the next step and you begin to sift through everything you hear and see. It sniffs out the things that you can use in your writing. What matters most is often hidden in plain sight.

Don't rush this step. Watch yourself with kindness and curiosity. Soon the writing practice that started out as ordinary – simply naming things – becomes extraordinary. It becomes a way of seeing things that connects your inner and outer landscapes. You wonder how you feel about it all, your responses to life and your writing process. And you start to trust your own opinion.

YOU START TO SEE LIFE AS AN ARTIST

The Naming Game is an excellent warm up for novelists. This writing meditation brings you into present time, and into the right mindset for your writing to flow.

A surprising benefit for writers, who usually live in their head so much, is you start to notice things that are out of place. And you find yourself editing your life with simple grace. In my bedroom, I just noticed a red Christmas tree bauble. It sits in a white egg cup that balances on a china seashell plate alongside a mossy twig, in the old fireplace. It's May, I've no idea why or how it got there. But it's time it went. I couldn't see it before, so it would never have occurred to me to write about it.

I think of what I want to say – and I just say it.

LINDEN MacINTYRE

TRY IT NOW. Set a timer for one minute. Look up. What do you see? Write three things that capture its soul. Do the exercise three times, get your eye in with broad deft strokes. Turn around, and do it again with a new view. What three things would a burglar notice?

LIFE LEAVES CLUES

The world is full of obvious things which nobody
by any chance ever observes.

ARTHUR CONAN DOYLE

The signature strength of The Naming Game is that it brings you into present time. This is essential if you are to write your best and it helps you to notice more in your every day. And as you stretch for the right name, you build the writing skills to put what you feel into your own words.

Robert McKee says a story is how you make sense out of life. Just as a champion learns by playing matches, a writer gets better only by actually writing.

THE EYE THAT NEVER SLEEPS

Rooms leave clues. How someone feels about their life. How they take up space in the world. What does your home say about you? Have a snoop around your home as if you're an uninvited detective whose motto is 'The Eye That Never Sleeps'. Ask yourself the type of questions you will ask of the characters in your story. Are you happy-go-lucky? Or an introvert? Distracted, careless? House-proud? How do you soothe your anxiety? With wine? Or bikes and sports equipment?

Have a go.

LIFE LEAVES CLUES GAME

Set a timer for ten minutes What does your home say about you? Nothing is too small to matter. Aim to inform your writing with the delight and curiosity of a child detective. When you enter a room or walk down a street, imagine that you are seeing it for the first time.

Who is this person?

What's their routine?

What would be their life motto?

Why does this person have so many/few books?

Take a book off a shelf. Why does this person own this book? Open the book at a random page and read a few lines – as if you are cracking the Enigma code. Who are they?

If you have a good idea for a story, don't assume it must form
a prose narrative. It may work better as a play, a screenplay
or a poem. Be flexible.

HILARY MANTEL

Set a timer for twenty minutes and write about your first memory of a childhood
bedroom. Write longhand. Feel your way back into the past.

YOUR MIND HOLIDAY

This morning, a friend FaceTimed me from a Portuguese island and showed me the translucent blue sea at first light. I was transported to her holiday. The beauty, the light, the pale lilac-green colour lit me up. I could feel it all on my skin. Close your eyes and recall a memory of a favourite holiday, ideally in nature. Imagine how its sights and sounds soothe and delight you. Then write for twenty minutes.

STARTER SENTENCE: I can feel…

WHAT'S THE SECRET TO DESCRIPT

> Description is what makes the reader a sensory participant in the story. Good description is a learned skill, one of the prime reasons why you cannot succeed unless you read a lot or write a lot. It's not just a question of how-to, you see: it's also a question of how much.
>
> STEPHEN KING

In real life, we bore others by saying too much. We bore them by not listening to their needs. It's the same with writing. A reader will put your book down if you bore them. The simple trick is to say less. Keep your reader listening out for more.

DON'T SPOON-FEED YOUR READER

Readers bring their own experiences to your writing, and they add stuff in their head. Leave room for their imagination to embroider your words. When you give them space to imagine, a reader customises your description, and this engages them more in your story, as an active listener. My fiction editor told me that very few writers know how to do this – so it's a great skill to pick up.

Stephen King says to pick three details your reader would notice if they walked into one of your settings. It's usually the first three things you see. My room has a row of bold, colourful seascapes above the kitchen sink, an IKEA ten-seater oak table, covered by an unfinished manuscript with neon-pink sticky notes. The kitchen wears espresso, like expensive old aftershave. The bright colours, the mess and the smell are the first three things you would notice.

WRITE YOUR DESCRIPTIONS AS A CHARACTER

Thinking about landscape as a character helps your descriptive writing to be more dynamic – instead of describing a passive backdrop, your landscape has a bigger role and a personality.

Ask yourself if your setting is a minor character or the antagonist? What role does your chosen landscape play? Ally or foe? The obstacle to your hero getting home? In the film *Gravity*, for example, space is the landscape-antagonist for a stranded astronaut.

REWRITE YOUR BEDROOM AS THE SETTING FOR A THRILLER

Setting is about context. What would your character notice? A child might notice your jewellery box. A killer might look for a weapon, and grab a heavy boot. Try this: turn your lights off and write by candlelight. What happens to the mood of the room? What happens in your imagination if you can't see in the dark? Set a timer for thirty minutes, and do a rough draft.

STARTER SENTENCE: I am looking at...

WHY WRITE LONGHAND?

All novelists write in a different way, but I always write in longhand
and then do two versions of typescript on a computer.

MARTIN AMIS

The advantage of writing by hand is that it slows you down to being in the moment. You connect your thoughts to your words. Your writing flows, because you are less tempted to stop and polish your words. There is something natural, conversational, about the writing of an author who writes longhand. It feels like you are in the narrator's head, and this is why so many authors are old school and do their first drafts longhand.

It works for J. K. Rowling, Neil Gaiman, Stephen King and Joyce Carol Oates, to name a few. You will be surprised how lovely it feels to write longhand.

NON-STOP FIRST DRAFT BY HAND

When you do something familiar – in a different way – it opens up more space in your mind. New ideas, fresh perspectives, more words and insights pop up, just when you thought you'd run out of steam. If writing by hand feels unfamiliar to you, start by writing longhand for your journal and your writing exercises. Brainstorming ideas and character sketches longhand will help you to switch to a more meditative mode if you've been on a screen all day.

Did I hear you say, you can't read your own handwriting? Me too. My handwriting is horrible. We get out of practice when we type all day. I had to slow down and show my words more respect.

Your longhand will improve when you're more present in the moment and write a line at a time. Give your handwriting some love, make it beautiful, experiment with different pens, maybe write with green ink. Writing is not about the grammar or your calligraphy. And it's not about what others think. It's about your awakening as a writer. A longhand first draft helps you to get there. Have a go.

WRITING PRACTICE

Making people believe the unbelievable is no trick; it's work. Belief and reader absorption come in the details. An overturned tricycle in the gutter of an abandoned neighborhood can stand for everything.

STEPHEN KING

PROMPT: An overturned tricycle in the gutter of an abandoned neighbourhood. Set a timer for twenty minutes; write more about Stephen King's idea. Think: Who? How? Why? What happened?

HOW CAN YOUR WRITING IMPROVE?

A word after a word after a word is power.

MARGARET ATWOOD

———————

You write in sentences. Line by line. This is so obvious that no one mentioned it on my Creative Writing MA. The tutors assumed we'd been taught how to write a sentence. I hadn't.

Even when we did a 'line-by-line edit' of our writing in a workshop, I didn't make the connection with writing sentences. I do hope you not are laughing at me. It's an embarrassing confession.

But we didn't speak about sentences; we spoke about writing as something mysterious, a huge wobbly mass of creative frogspawn: no clear end, no beginning, hard to pick up, prone to slip through your fingers when you try to catch it. Writing could feel elitist, something that only 'born' writers are any good at.

———————

WRITE IN SENTENCES

But pay attention to your sentences, and your writing can take care of itself; sentence by sentence. A bit like that old saying, save your pennies and the pounds take care of themselves.

Sentences are your building blocks, the foundations for your book. The stage on which your words shine or stink or, worse, confuse and bore your reader.

And you can feel a sense of accomplishment when you finish one sentence. Empowered, you can write the next one, the next, and the next. Endless small wins that release dopamine.

You learn to hear how your words stitch together, how your words flow or stutter, and you juggle them into a poem, or they inspire a scene for a novel.

You improve by writing. Set a timer for twenty minutes. Write about a time you were disappointed.

STARTER SENTENCE: The time I…

WORKSHOP YOURSELF

How did you respond? What did you notice? In a writing workshop, one of the most useful skills you learn is called a 'Reflective Commentary'. You reflect and write about your own writing. A writing workshop is like good journaling; it's curious and non-judgemental. Astonishing insights can occur when you ask yourself: What am I trying to say here in my writing?

START WITH ONE SENTENCE

All you have to do is write one true sentence. Write the truest sentence that you know. So finally I would write one true sentence, and then go on from there. It was easy then because there was always one true sentence that I knew or had seen or had heard someone say.

ERNEST HEMINGWAY

In his passion project *First You Write A Sentence*, Professor Joe Moran tells the story of a legendary American creative writing professor who only allowed his graduate students to write one sentence in class for a whole year. After a year, they were allowed to write two sentences.

The idea is for your mind to slow down and connect to your writing.

Take time to find what you love about your sentences. Learn to write a sentence that pleases you. Practise writing before you grapple with story rather than the other way round. Doing things in the right order, at the right time, avoids bad habits and muddles. You will enjoy writing more.

And, further down the road, when someone asks you to pitch your whole story in one sentence – known as a logline – you will find it easier to write a great sentence.

WORKSHOP YOURSELF

What matters the most to you in your writing? Example: Do you care more about theme than character? French novelist, Gustave Flaubert cared most about the rhythm, wit and beauty of his sentences in *Madamé Bovary*, but it was his scandalous story of adultery that made it into a bestseller.

WRITE ONE SENTENCE

Write one sentence about your pet stalking a squirrel — or your pet talking to a squirrel!

_____

Write one sentence about how you make a sandwich for the Queen.

_____

Write one sentence about how you would climb a tree.

_____

Write one sentence about you.

_____

Write one more sentence.

THE REPETITION GAME

Moments of pure inspiration are glorious, but most of a writer's life is, to adapt the old cliché, about perspiration rather than inspiration. Sometimes you have to write even when the muse isn't cooperating.

J. K. ROWLING

A champion tennis coach explained to me that you must practise for a minimum of three hours to every lesson or you won't improve your tennis playing. It's great advice for writing too. Go back to The Naming Game practice. Set a timer for one minute. Look up, and describe where you are. Repeat this exercise six times – get your eye in with broad deft strokes. Turn around, and do it again with a different view. What three things would a burglar notice?

PROMPT: I am looking at…

I am looking at…

I am looking at…

I am looking at…

I am looking at…

I am looking at…

When you do this *I am looking at* writing practice, expand your awareness and notice how people are speaking. Listen to the teenagers on the bus, make a point of having a walk when the schools come out. Watch people. Watch their relationships. How people touch each other tells you how they feel. Does your family greet each other with a hug or a peck on the cheek?

WHAT BRINGS YOU TO WRITING?

The best time to plan a book is while you're doing the dishes.

AGATHA CHRISTIE

What brings you to writing now? Why do you want to write? When you know your purpose – your WHY, the reason you want to write – you can leave your warm bed on a cold morning to do it. Set a timer for twenty-five minutes and see if you can coax your purpose out. You need this as a compass to steer your writing life.

STARTER SENTENCE: I want to write because…

WHAT DO YOU WANT TO ACHIEVE?

We are very different creatures at different times in our lives. A twenty-year-old might be fired by ambition and want to write The Great American Novel. A sixty-year-old might be more reflective, value balance in their life, and want to write poetry. What do you want to write? A song? A memoir? A novel? Or do you have a burning story to tell? Do you write to know life better?

WHAT is one thing you can do to achieve this today? This week? This year? Try this. Set yourself a weekly word count: 1,500–2,000 words? Can you manage one scene a week? That's a first draft of a novel in six months.

WHEN are you going to write? HOW can you make that happen? Do you save Netflix, nights out, as a treat for the weekend? Bed at 10pm. Get up early? What is one thing you can do?

WHERE ARE YOU GOING TO WRITE?

Your environment matters – it can help or hinder your progress. What is one thing you can do to encourage your working space to support you?

TIP
A yoga mat makes a superb temporary workspace to pin up scenes and ideas. It helps to see your story visually. My yoga mat is covered with a hundred coloured sticky notes. When my husband kicks off about the mess on the kitchen table, I simply roll it up. And I can take it to the park.

THE REWARD JAR GAME

Reward your support team. How this works: Every fifteen minutes that no one interrupts your writing practice, you drop coins or brightly painted pasta into a small jar. The trick is to be really generous; the intention to PRAISE. PRAISE. PRAISE.

Double rewards when you keep your word to yourself and write.

Triple rewards when you resist the urge to cook tea or do housework on your night 'off'.

When the jar is full, reward everyone with a weekly treat. Encourage children and flatmates to support you. The reward can be anything from a game to a movie night with popcorn, snuggled under a blanket together. Phones off. Give them the gift of your attention. Make this a joyful ritual with your friends and family that celebrates your writing practice.

READERS HEAR YOUR WORDS

I know nothing in the world that has as much power as a word.
Sometimes I write one, and I look at it, until it begins to shine.

EMILY DICKINSON

It is harder than you think to write a good sentence, isn't it? How do you know what a good sentence and good writing sound like anyway? The options are endless. 'Hello!' is a one-word sentence, which breaks the rule that a sentence must have an object and a verb. Rules can confuse. Here are five simple rules from Professor Joe Moran to help you create music in your writing.

1. Use short words – they sound more emotional.

2. Shorten your sentences – for clarity.

3. Vary your sentence length – for rhythm.

4. Use more verbs – verbs are action words so they move your story forward.

5. Try accumulative sentences. In a long sentence, put your main verb close to the top of your sentence, in a short clause, and then you can add more and more clauses without your reader getting lost.

THE WORDS OF SOUND

The power of sound has always been greater than the power of sense.

JOSEPH CONRAD

A reader *hears* your words in their head when they read your writing. And if you want your writing to *sound* better, use more short words because vowels carry the *emotion* in a word.

Take a moment to fully appreciate this truth. Reading is as much about hearing as seeing.

VOWELS CARRY EMOTION IN WRITING

This is the reason that poets use short words. And why opera singers will warm up by singing only vowel sounds – they want to maximise emotion in their voice.

SHORT WORDS = EMOTION

How does this work? When you read, you emphasise one vowel sound in each word, no matter how long that word is. Multisyllable words might look impressive, but a reader still stresses only one vowel sound in each word – which means lengthy words emit less feeling. You get more bang for your buck with short words, because you create more vowel sounds on every page.

TIP
Let your writing unfold in the present moment.

Most of us spend a lot of time censoring everything that we see and hear. Does it fit with our world picture? And if it doesn't, how can we shut it out, how can we ignore it, how can we challenge it?

JEANETTE WINTERSON

What stories did you hear that shaped your view of the world? Pick one and rework it.

Set a timer for twenty minutes and write longhand.

PROMPT: I imagine ...

THE POWER OF SHORT WORDS

Memorise David Whyte's poem (below). It tells you everything you need to know about how to write. And how to live. Read it so often that you can hear its words whenever you get stuck, so you recall its wisdom to start close in on your writing.

Start Close In

Start close in,
don't take the second step
or the third,
start with the first
thing
close in,
the step
you don't want to take.

Start with
the ground
you know,
the pale ground
beneath your feet,
your own
way to begin
the conversation.

Start with your own
question,
give up on other
people's questions,
don't let them
smother something
simple.

To hear
another's voice,
follow
your own voice,
wait until
that voice
becomes a private ear
that can
really listen
to another.
Start right now
take a small step
you can call you own
don't follow
someone else's
heroics, be humble
and focused,
start close in,
don't mistake
that other
for your own.

Start close in,
don't take
the second step
or the third,
start with the first
thing
close in,
the step
you don't want to take.

THE MASTERPIECE GAME

A feminist is anyone who recognizes the equality
and full humanity of women and men.

GLORIA STEINEM

Write another verse of the poem. Copy David Whyte's poem out by hand, and keep going with your own verse. This practice teaches you to use tools before you forget them. Be in the moment. Curious. Set a timer for half an hour, just to get you out the door. Take the first step.

PROMPT: What is the step you don't want to take?

WORKSHOP YOURSELF

What do you think? Somehow, this wonderful poem makes me feel broken, and alive. The simple, short words call you to take action.

Do you see how good writing is possible for you too?

WHY VARY YOUR SENTENCE LENGTHS?

Nothing in life is more important than the ability
to communicate effectively.

GERALD FORD

When you vary sentence lengths, you create rhythm. Your writing sings. Gary Provost gets this idea across brilliantly in his poem of a paragraph.

> This sentence has five words. Here are five more words. Five-word sentences are fine. But several together become monotonous. Listen to what is happening. The writing is getting boring. The sound of it drones. It's like a stuck record. The ear demands some variety. Now listen. I vary the sentence length, and I create music. Music. The writing sings. It has a pleasant rhythm, a lilt, a harmony.
>
> GARY PROVOST, *100 Ways To Improve Your Writing*

Need I say more?

This is why you vary your sentence lengths: for the pleasing rhythm it creates. And from neuroscience, we know that rhythm is one of the core ways that you calm and self-regulate your mind and body.

Have a go, because this one simple trick will elevate your writing effortlessly. Every time.

Style is a very simple matter: it is all *rhythm*.

VIRGINIA WOOLF

Take a piece of your own writing. Write it out – word for word – by hand. But start each sentence on a new line so you can see their lengths. Now look at it again. Can you see the *shape* of your writing better? Can you hear its rhythm? Churchill wrote his best speeches this way. He began a new line for each sentence to check their length. And he read them aloud to hear the rhythm to stir up patriotic emotion in wartime. This trick still works, if the ONLY thing you do in your writing is to *alternate* your sentence lengths. One long sentence, one short. The Morse Code of rhythm. It's foolproof. Emotion is what persuades people – not facts.

This is a really useful tip.

WORKSHOP YOURSELF

What did you notice about this exercise? How did you respond to it?

THE SENTENCE GAME

I will not have my life narrowed down. I will not bow down to
someone else's whim or someone else's ignorance.

BELL HOOKS

Read this extract from Greta Thunberg's 2019 Action Summit speech to the
United Nations. Note how she varies her sentence lengths and uses short
words. Be brave. Read it aloud with passion.

This is all wrong.
I shouldn't be up here.
I should be back in school on the other side of the ocean.
Yet you all come to us young people for hope.
How dare you!
You have stolen my dreams and my childhood with your empty words.
And yet I'm one of the lucky ones.
People are suffering.
People are dying.
Entire ecosystems are collapsing.
We are in the beginning of a mass extinction, and all you can talk about is
money and fairy tales of eternal economic growth.

How dare you!
For more than thirty years, the science has been crystal clear.
How dare you continue to look away and come here saying that you're doing
enough, when the politics and solutions needed are still nowhere in sight.
You say you hear us and that you understand the urgency.
But no matter how sad and angry I am, I do not want to believe that.
Because if you really understood the situation and still kept on failing to act,
then you would be evil.
And that I refuse to believe.

Greta Thunberg has an autism spectrum disorder called Asperger's, but she knows that people care more about the emotion and the sound of her words than the actual science. How can you use this idea in your own writing?

WHAT MAKES YOU ANGRY?

The What makes you angry? question generates ideas and shows you what you really care about. Ask yourself: What is making me mad this week? Even something small, like feeling frustrated that you have no time to write, will give you an idea for a scene in a story. Start with a list.

SCRIBBLE YOUR LIST HERE:

Now write your own speech for something that matters to you. Keep your idea simple. Do not procrastinate by doing research. It could be an impassioned teenager lecturing Dad. Or a scene about an adult in denial. Set a timer for thirty minutes and write from the heart – make it as emotional as you can – and read it aloud to hear the rhythm: a speech is spoken word.

THE LISTENING GAME

If you are using dialogue – say it aloud as you write it. Only then will it have the sound of speech.

JOHN STEINBECK

Try this exercise while lying on the ground. You can train yourself to hear the rhythm in your writing by listening to music. Stop whatever else you are doing and listen to Chopin's piano Nocturnes Op 9 No 2. Eavesdrop on its magic, the simple individual notes, hear the wonder in the silence between them. Imagine writing music for a human voice.

WORKSHOP YOURSELF

What happened? Did you do the exercise? How do your words sound? A whisper, loud, strong, short, long, fast, slow? How can you bring musicality into your writing?

We often forget that the sky is a landscape too. Try this. Go outside to write. Breathe; find the words to capture that feeling in the weather.

Set a timer for ten minutes. Write three sentences about the sky at different times of day, weather conditions and location.

THEY SAY MY WRITING IS CONFUSING

It is a great privilege to make one's living from writing sentences.
The sentence is the greatest invention of civilization.

JOHN BANVILLE

Okay, take a break. Go for a walk before the next bit. Your head is spinning with possibilities for how you can light up your writing. It's a lot to take in. This last point requires a fresh, open mind.

You need to be able to write complex ideas with clarity. The trick is to smash an 'accumulative sentence'. It sounds a mouthful, but it just means 'bit by bit'. Research on the top non-fiction writers, found that over 50% of their sentences were accumulative. Think of this kind of sentence as a train, powered by an engine, with carriages tugging along behind.

- The engine is your main verb. For clarity, put it close to the top, in a short clause.

- This *drives* the sentence forward, because the verb tells the reader what the sentence is about.

- Then *add* as many other clauses, or carriages, as you like. No one gets left behind. Or lost.

- Start small: add more. Watch your writing fly with clarity, and beauty.

> EXAMPLE: from *Hamnet* by Maggie O'Farrell
>
> The room is empty, the fire ruminating in its grate, orange embers below slow, spiralling smoke. His injured kneecaps throb in time with his heartbeat. He stands with one hand resting on the latch of the door to the stairs, the scuffed leather tip of his boot raised, poised for motion, for flight.

WRITING PRACTICE

Every worthwhile accomplishment, big or little, has its stages of
drudgery and triumph: a beginning, a struggle, and a victory.

MAHATMA GANDHI

An accumulative sentence takes practice until, like driving a car, you can do it
on auto-pilot. Take it slowly at the start. The main verb is your engine: put it close
to the top, in a short clause, and you can add as many other clauses as you like,
(the bit between commas) without a reader getting lost.

EXAMPLE:

The coffee pot *exploded* across the desk, flooding her notebooks, brown
gritty stains bloomed over the manuscript, the dark bog spun and swirled
the pens and a pendulum, before it encircled her laptop, and dripped off
the edge onto mother's cream carpet.

PROMPT: Look up, what do you see? Pick one thing to write about in an
accumulative sentence.

PRACTISE. PRACTISE. PRACTISE. Do three more accumulative sentences.

What do you think? Getting the hang of it? Take a break from it now and let the skill grow naturally.

IT'S ALL IN THE DETAIL

Take The Naming Game up another notch with this exercise. Be specific. Writing comes alive with detail. This is the opening sentence of *Gods and Warriors* by Michelle Paver.

The shaft of the arrow was black and fletched with crow feathers, but Hylas couldn't see the head because it was buried in his arm.

TRY THIS:

Copy it out by hand right now to get a real feel for her words, or you will be tempted to skim read this sentence. And it probably took Michelle Paver, a writer who loves to plan out everything, months to perfect it.

How did you respond to it?

How layered do you think this sentence is?

How hard is the description of the arrow working?

Michelle Paver gives the child reader an immersive experience. You feel what the protagonist is feeling. This line is compressed, no wasted words, but it creates action and tension.

The detail takes a game and places it in a time when you got shot at for real with bows and arrows – this is wish fulfilment for children who long to live wild.

Paver holds back the surprise – the hook – to the end of the sentence, so you are curious to read on about a boy with an arrow buried in his arm. Ouch.

TIP
This week, visit a bookshop and head for your favourite section. Soak up the magic.

There was a hand in the darkness, and it held a knife.

NEIL GAIMAN

PROMPT: Write the opening sentence to a children's book. Play. Throw your words at the page.

THE SURPRISING THINGS WRITING NEEDS

Does this path have a heart? If the answer is no, you will know it, and then you must choose another path.

CARLOS CASTANEDA

Writing needs content and form, or structure. A simple way to think about them is like this: Content is emotion. Structure is thought.

CONTENT IS EMOTION? WHAT!!!?

Okay. Stop, right here. We will talk about structure later, but 'content is emotion' sounds fridge-magnet profound. How did you react? Did it stop you in your tracks? It would me. I'd wonder what on earth that meant, but I'd dare not ask, for fear of looking foolish. Or did you turn it over like a pebble in your mind, excited? This simple idea has such potential for your writing; take a moment and let it sink in. Have you woken up to the magic that lies ahead and inside you?

To create content, think about yourself and the people in your life. What do they care about? How and why do they respond to things as they do? You take what is specific to you and find that it has universal appeal. You have so much content in your life that finding ideas for stories is not going to be a problem.

WORK YOUR OWN EMOTIONS FOR CONTENT

People's emotions are rarely put into words, far more often they are expressed through other cues. The key to intuiting another's feelings is in the ability to read nonverbal channels, tone of voice, gesture, facial expressions and the like.

DANIEL GOLEMAN

The craft of writing has many layers. But the same writing tools do more complex things. Try The Naming Game on your feelings. Observe yourself, name your emotion. This is surprisingly hard to do.

FBI hostage negotiators are highly trained in emotional intelligence. They use a technique called 'labelling'. They NAME your emotions for you to defuse a situation. You feel seen, less defensive. To be clear, this is not 'labelling' as judgement, calling someone racist etc., but as in, *'I see you'.*

This works when you do it on yourself. The trick is not to ask yourself a direct question such as 'Why are you so angry?' An FBI negotiator would say 'It seems like you're feeling angry?' This softer question makes you reflect, and think: yeah, now you mention it, I am feeling peed off, I wonder why? Then, hey presto, you have caught a tadpole of emotional content that you can write into a song, a scene, a novel, or family memoir. The added benefit? When you bring awareness to a negative emotion it helps you to release it. Once you can name your feelings, they feel seen and you can let go. No judgement or action required.

THE GOOD NEWS

When you name a positive emotion, it reinforces your good mood. You get a hit of dopamine.

PROMPT: How do you feel about writing today?

THE STOP & CHECK-IN GAME

Set a timer on the hour to do a STOP and CHECK-IN – this means you name your emotion in that moment. Are you angry, sad, happy, bored, afraid, distracted, excited, absent-minded, stressed, chilled? Notice how your body feels when you pinpoint your emotion and listen to what it is saying. Why? Because this practice makes you more self-aware and skilled as a writer. Have a go.

PROMPT: it seems like/feels like/sounds like/looks like/I am feeling…

TIP
Always carry a small notebook with you. Make a note of something that catches your attention. A notebook doesn't need to be fancy. Choreographer Twyla Tharp keeps an index card and pencil in her back pocket – they are light – and a pencil doesn't leak in your bag.

THE CHARACTER CHECK-IN

STOP and CHECK-IN with your characters as you write – observe and label how they're feeling in a scene. Otherwise, look up. Who do you see? Write about the first person you see.

PROMPT: it seems like/feels like/sounds like/looks like they are feeling....

THE 100 MOMENTS GAME

Fill your paper with the breathings of your heart.

WILLIAM WORDSWORTH

Let's sweep up some content from your life. Nothing is too small to matter.

List 100 moments from your life; anything from a sibling joke to your first kiss. Start small, go after the brighter moments that jump out at you. Once you start, more memories will unlock. Examples: Granny heating your red wine in a microwave, the smell of tadpoles, a grass snake caught under the caravan door, the way your mother put on lipstick, your aunt's china cup, watching the clouds.

Set a timer for thirty minutes. Write fast, longhand. Look for content with heart; small, happy moments. Let it flow. Capture each memory in one line. You can get the meat off the bone later.

1

2

3

4

5

6

7

8

9

10

11

12
13
14
15
16
17
18
19
20
21
22
23
24
25
26
27
28
29
30
31
32
33
34

35

36

37

38

39

40

41

42

43

44

45

46

47

48

49

50

51

52

53

54

55

56

57

58

59

60

61

62

63

64

65

66

67

68

69

70

71

72

73

74

75

76

77

78

79

80

81

82

83

84

85

86

87

88

89

90

91

92

93

94

95

96

97

98

99

100

Well done. Now get some scissors.

THE PROMPT GAME

We are what we pretend to be, so we must be careful
about what we pretend to be.

KURT VONNEGUT

Close your eyes and stab your finger on the 100-prompt list. Write more about
that thing. Give yourself no choice or you will dither. Set a timer for fifteen minutes. Breathe yourself back into the past. Remember to write longhand. If you
haven't done your 100 list, write about how you felt on your first day at work.

STARTER SENTENCE: I remember…

PROMPT YOURSELF

Do one thing every day that scares you.

ELEANOR ROOSEVELT

The hardest thing for a writer to do is to actually start writing. It feels like anything goes in writing, and this can overwhelm you. Too much choice.

A writing prompt works by drastically limiting your choice so you can write without dithering. In class, a tutor does this for you by giving you a specific prompt, it could be to write about a shoe or how your big toe feels. The topic doesn't matter. What matters is that everything else drops away, you can focus on that one prompt, and write.

AMBUSH YOURSELF

The way to do this for yourself is to create an unexpected prompt. Otherwise, you will scan the 100 list, faff about which idea to pick, and your inner critic will pop in with their pennyworth.

The trick is to print off the 100 list, cut out each moment, fold each one up and pop them all into a Sorting Hat. Or a prompt box. Pick one, commit to it, and use this moment as your prompt.

Do the same thing when you get stuck for an idea in a novel. Pick one moment, write about the emotion it evokes.

You will find that this works like dominoes – a memory seems light, almost insubstantial, but as you write about it, momentum builds until it packs such a punch it can knock over much bigger objects. One single moment off your 100 list can open a door to your past.

MAKE A PROMPT BOX

Find a box, print off your 100 list, cut out each moment, fold them up and pop them in the box. Top them up every week. Prompts are everywhere – a word you love, an unusual name, something you see on TV. Keep your prompt box full of surprises – a toy car, a twig, a stone, a tin of sardines – and you will always have something to write about. Dip your hand in the box, pull out a prompt and write about it. The trick is to write about that particular thing, and not fish for a 'better' one. This constraint gives you more freedom to write.

PROMPT: What would happen if a person found a baby hidden under a scarecrow in a deserted field?

DRESS-UP GAME: IS THIS ME?

Acting is the least mysterious of all crafts. Whenever we want
something from somebody or when we want to hide something or
pretend, we're acting. Most people do it all day long.

MARLON BRANDO

You thrive when you feel like you belong. You need to find that sense of belonging for your writing. Your identity differs from your personality and from your character.

Writers often seek a writing identity to fit in with others. You are wired to fit in, and it is natural to do this. You compare yourself with other writers. You worry what 'good' writing looks like.

But what if you can find your own way? It helps to get out of your head, and look at how you make writing choices through a different lens. Your body is a great writing barometer. That inner feeling of 'this is me' is what you are after in your writing. It helps to build this muscle from things that you are already highly skilled in.

This writing exercise is based around the Dress-Up Game. This is as childish as it seems. You play dress-up games as a child. One moment you're a bus driver, the next a king. This game is serious work – you try on different outfits to seek your true identity. You still do this unconsciously.

Example: How do you pick an outfit for a smart work party?

• Do you pick your clothes to fit in with your friends or to impress them?

• Do you turn up at a party and check the room to see if you are over- or under-dressed, and find you can't enjoy the moment?

- Or do you choose the clothes that you *feel* your best in? That are the most 'you'? Then it doesn't matter what everyone else is wearing because being you is more important to you.

IS THIS ME?

The Dress-Up Game is simply to be mindful of how you pick your clothes for a week.

The poet John O'Donohue said your body is your soul's only home on Earth. Your body is sacred.

Check in with yourself when you dress. This is not about a perfect figure. Writing confidence comes the same way, honouring yourself.

The questions you might ask yourself are: Do I feel good in this? Is this me? Go for what feels *right*.

WORKSHOP YOURSELF

What did you notice? When I road-tested this exercise, I realised how unconsciously I dress to fit in. Or else anything goes when I work from home. But what I really love is colour, natural fabrics, and well-cut clothes. What do you love?

Could you get your head around the idea your body is sacred? Did you take time to consider how you want clothes to feel? Did you check in with yourself via your body? Did you notice how it brings you into present time? How you feel more at home with yourself? Can you find a feeling of being at ease with yourself, no matter what size or shape or age you are? How can you bring this ease to writing, no matter what stage you are at? What's the most 'you'?

Set a timer for thirty minutes, and write longhand, without stopping.

STARTER SENTENCE: I noticed...

WHAT IF IT'S ALL BEEN DONE? WHAT IS ORIGINAL?

Do you know what I learned from writing *How We Die*, if I learned nothing else? The more personal you are willing to be about the details of your own life, the more universal you are...

DR SHERWIN NULAND

It is easy to confuse novelty with originality: context makes the content in your work original.

This is another of those huge points that look simple and easy to dismiss when you are hunting for the Big Idea – context transforms your writing. Often, what you're looking for is under your nose.

A specific context can give you a fresh take on universal emotions – love, fear, jealousy, hate, revenge, anger, shame, losing face, courage, grief, hope.

> EXAMPLE:
>
> Mother love is universal – but the circumstances of a mother in Aleppo are different from a mother in Chicago. Everything changes with context.

YOUR OWN CONTEXT MAKES
YOUR CONTENT ORIGINAL

Start with the context of your own life.

As a writer, you have an enormous gift to notice and question your own life in its small details. These small details shape who you are. Your life might *seem* ordinary, but it's not. You are an original. A complete one-off. Appreciate the singularity of your life; no one else has your unique experiences and take on life.

Want proof? Who would you be if you had been born next door? Think about this. Just one door over, and you would have had different parents, a different family history with different values and opinions, different struggles and different opportunities. Different DNA.

What if you changed the order of your birth, becoming the eldest child not the youngest? What if your parents were born in a different era? How would that change how you see life?

See how little it takes to make up a completely different story?

This is context.

BORN NEXT DOOR GAME

We discover who we are often by contrast, by realising who we are not. Take an hour for this exercise. Explore it on the page. Who would you be if you changed one thing about yourself? Or imagine your character's childhood if they were born elsewhere.

PROMPT: Who would you be…?

THE INTERVIEW GAME

When people talk, listen completely. Most people never listen.

ERNEST HEMINGWAY

You need content to write. Ideas are everywhere. Listen to how other people talk and you will hear their stories and get an endless supply of ideas. Start close in on your own life and interview your mother. Ask her what kind of person she was before she had children. What were her hopes and dreams? If, like me, you've lost one or both parents, interview a person who is significant to you.

PROMPT: List their key stories here…

I always listen to what I can leave out.

MILES DAVIS

Take one of your mother's stories. Explore the story with your pen. What comes up for you? Does the story reshape how you see your mother? Set a timer for thirty minutes, and write.

PROMPT: I notice...

HOW DO YOU WRITE DIALOGUE?

Dialogue is a lean language in which every word counts.

SOL STEIN

The trick to writing good dialogue is to understand that it is 'heightened' reality. You don't copy how people ramble on and on in real life, in a story. Good dialogue is as much form as it is content.

Structure your dialogue as action/reaction.

Give it a goal. Give it an opponent.

That said, be careful of taking screenwriting advice on dialogue in a novel. The language of film is visual, non-verbal. Dialogue is the last thing a professional screenwriter writes in their screenplay.

Novelists often start with dialogue and write in the first person to find their character. The danger of this is you get too attached to your dialogue. This makes it hard to cut your darlings when they don't serve your story. Good dialogue moves your story forward. Be ruthless, cut waffle.

SUBTEXT
People rarely say what they mean. Listen out for The Thing they really want to say.
This conflict often lies underneath what they say. Example: An unkind sister might say, 'New outfit? You're never going out on a first date in that?'

PROMPT: Write a conversation between two sisters sorting through their late mother's belongings, who both want her ring. Who are they? Where are they? What do they say to keep/get the ring?

THE DIALOGUE GAME

All the information you need can be given in dialogue.

ELMORE LEONARD

Turn your headphones off and listen to the world. Bring The Naming Game, and your observational skills, to your ears. Do this on the bus, at work, in shops. Eavesdrop on children.

TRAIN YOURSELF TO HEAR WHAT MATTERS TO OTHER PEOPLE

List seven snippets of overheard conversation. Hear what matters to other people. Example: An angry dad saying 'If you don't stop crying, I'll give you something to cry about.'

1

2

3

4

5

6

7

DIALOGUE PRACTICE

Now set a timer for ten minutes. Pick one snippet of your overheard conversations and write more about it. Feel your way into the emotions of the people you observed.

POINT OF VIEW

Of course I am not worried about intimidating men. The type of man who will be intimidated by me is exactly the type of man I have no interest in.

CHIMAMANDA NGOZI ADICHIE

POV is shorthand for the Point of View of your narrator/character. It reminds you to be specific when you write dialogue. A three-year-old would notice different things in a room and talk about them in a very different way than your character's mother. A playful child might see jewellery as a dressing up game, but a mum sees the dirty dishes hidden under the sofa, and picks them up, which leaves your character feeling either judged, or grateful, depending on their relationships.

PROMPT: Write about the time someone barged into your room uninvited.

WHY READING INSPIRES WRITING

You should write because you love the shape of stories and sentences and the creation of different words on a page. Writing comes from reading, and reading is the finest teacher of how to write.

ANNIE PROULX

As a writer, you walk on roads that others built. If you don't read, you might find your own way, but you won't go as far as you could. Imitation is a natural step in the writing process: how you learn to raise your game without having to reinvent the wheel every time. This approach to skill learning is accepted as perfectly normal in other spheres of the arts.

I trained as a fine artist. I learned to draw by copying original Raphael and Leonardo da Vinci drawings in the Ashmolean Museum in Oxford. I redrew these masterpieces, mark by mark, trying to capture the vigour of their lines. It's great practice to train your eye. And your ear. You are listening to what the artist is saying. Ernest Hemingway would write in Parisian cafes in the morning and take his lunch to the museum to study the Cézannes. Hemingway tended to his artist's eye in order to nurture his writing.

READING IS HOW YOU TEACH YOURSELF TO WRITE BETTER

Reading is an essential practice for a writer. The trick to heightened reading skills is to copy down the words of another writer. This helps you to understand how they write. I'm not suggesting that you steal or plagiarise other writers' words in your own creative writing. This is an exercise in reading and understanding.

You will find your own way. But first you need to recognise and trust your preferences.

Ask questions: I wonder why they did it this way? You see what you can emulate for your own work, and what you reject as not being you. This practice gives you vital information about your emerging voice. And it shows you how and what you can improve upon.

Grab your coat and this book and go for a walk. Sit under a tree and read the next bit.

THE IMITATION GAME

Read this text from *I Capture The Castle* by Dodie Smith. I'll explain why in a moment.

I write this sitting in the kitchen sink. That is, my feet are in it; the rest of me is on the draining-board, which I have padded with our dog's blanket and the tea-cosy. I can't say that I am really comfortable, and there is a depressing smell of carbolic soap, but this is the only part of the kitchen where there is any daylight left. And I have found that sitting in a place where you have never sat before can be inspiring — I wrote my very best poem on the hen-house. Though even that isn't a very good poem. I have decided my poetry is so bad that I mustn't write any more of it.

Drips from the roof are plopping into the water-butt by the back door. The view through the windows above the sink is excessively drear. Beyond the dank garden in the courtyard are the ruined walls on the edge of the moat. Beyond the moat, the boggy ploughed fields stretch to the leaden sky. I tell myself that all the rain we have had lately is good for nature, and that at any moment spring will surge on us. I try to see leaves on the trees and the courtyard filled with sunlight. Unfortunately, the more my mind's eye sees green and gold, the more drained of all colour does the twilight seem.

It is comforting to look away from the windows and towards the kitchen fire, near which my sister Rose is ironing — though she obviously can't see properly, and it will be a pity if she scorches her only nightgown. (I have two, but one is minus its behind.) Rose looks particularly fetching by firelight because she is a pinkish gold, very light and feathery. Although I am rather used to her I know she is a beauty. She is nearly twenty-one and very bitter with life. I am seventeen, look younger, feel older. I am no beauty but have a neatish face.

The best way to learn to write is by reading. Reading critically, noticing paragraphs that get the job done, how your favourite writers use verbs, all the useful techniques. A scene catches you? Go back and study it. Find out how it works.

TONY HILLERMAN

TASK

Copy the opening page to *I Capture the Castle*, word for word. Pay great attention to each word. The exact punctuation. Take this slowly. Do it with reverence and appreciation. Trust me, it's worth the effort.

What do you notice when you do a close read of another writer?

How can you use it?

What do you understand so far about the story?

Ask yourself how you would do it differently.

I Capture the Castle by Dodie Smith has an iconic opening line. It might comfort you to know that this brilliant playwright-turned-author, who later wrote *The Hundred and One Dalmatians*, agonised over every line, and once she finished the novel, she spent two years editing it; she couldn't sleep at night, *worrying if it was any good*. It was an overnight hit and remains in print after five decades.

Write about a person in a kitchen who feels life is passing them by. Is their home an antagonist? An obstacle? Or is it the safe harbour in their life? If you get stuck, start by listing what your character is looking at in their kitchen. How does it make them feel?

WHAT DO THEY DO?

I go to a beauty salon and have my hair blown dry.
It's cheaper by far than psychoanalysis, and much more uplifting.

NORA EPHRON

For this exercise, find a writer whose work you love and copy a page of their work down here. What do you notice? What do you notice about their writing when you pay closer attention?

NO TIME TO READ?

We read books to find out who we are. What other people, real or imaginary, do and think and feel... is an essential guide to our understanding of what we ourselves are and may become.

URSULA LE GUIN

If you don't have time to read, stop doing something else. Save Netflix for the weekends. When you are really time poor a *close* read of just one page of a book is excellent practice. The added benefit is you are training your eye for when you come to critique other writers' work. Appreciate what they are trying to do in their writing before your point out their mistakes.

When you read a chapter of a book, notice when you skim over descriptive passages.

What made you lose interest?

What sparked your interest?

What can you use in your own writing? Take one sentence that you particularly love and rewrite it in your own words. Read it out loud, pay attention to its rhythm. What appeals to you about it?

BOOKS ARE YOUR LIFELINE

Make reading fun. Integrate it into your life.

Read aloud to your partner, read to your mother.

Ask children to read aloud to you while you cook supper.

Ask for an audiobook subscription for your birthday.

Share the love. Reading with others creates empathy and closeness. Just read.

WHAT HAVE YOU DISCOVERED?

Until I feared I would lose it, I never loved to read.
One does not love breathing.

HARPER LEE

Practise what you learn before you move on to learn something new. Or it won't stick.

- How did you get on? Did you do The Naming Game exercises?

- What happened when you interviewed your mother?

- Have you found other family stories?

- How do you like the sounds of your sentences?

- Do you make time to read and write?

- Can you manage a close read of a page every other day?

- Did you find a few precious hours a week to write?

- What is your writing about?

What have you discovered about your writing so far?

Go back through the book and highlight what spoke to you. List your insights in the YOUR WORKBOOK HIGHLIGHTS at the end of the book. You worked so hard; it would be a waste to lose your unique insights. Go and capture them. Next time you get stuck, you'll have all your best tools in one place at the back of this book.

ACT TWO

SURVIVE

A LITTLE KNOW-HOW SAVES
YOU A LOT OF BOTHER

SURVIVAL SKILLS

Your job as a writer is to make sense out of life.

ROBERT McKEE

You can survive anything when you know: Who you are. What you want. How to do it.

You might write because a glorious urge captures your heart and mind. You want to write a book, but get stuck when you don't know how to do it. When we are lost, some basic survival skills come in very handy. It seems counter-intuitive, but in the wilderness your priority is to find shelter over food. You must protect yourself from the environment.

HOME

The most dangerous place for writing is often your own head. Fear can snuff out a bonfire of great ideas and inspiration. Writing needs shelter, a place of belonging, where you feel welcome and accepted unconditionally, with no fears about being sent packing if you make a mistake. But when you are uncertain, a mouse-sized threat will look big in the shadows. And you freeze to keep safe. Small obstacles, over time, can cause excoriating, seemingly insurmountable, writer's blocks.

My garden sink overflowed with stormwater. The plughole was blocked. I cleared away a few leaves and watched as the rainwater gushed down the drain. It struck me how writing blocks can often be small things; obstacles, fears that feel too silly to mention, but they cause a lot of bother.

INNER HYGIENE

Declutter old stories and unhelpful beliefs from your mind. This creates more space for you to be creative. Anthropologist Jean Houston calls silencing your inner critic 'inner hygiene'. It's the same idea as The Naming Game but you look inside to sense and observe yourself. What stories are you telling yourself that do not serve you? What scares you? How do you react to things? You don't try to fix old things. You declutter. Acknowledge stuff. And let it go. It's done its time. Inner hygiene is a lifelong practice. Release nonsense with kindness. Smile when stuff comes back, which it will. The Second Law of Thermodynamics says chaos always returns. Unless you keep it in order.

INNER HYGIENE GAME

You are not a passive observer in the cosmos. The entire universe is expressing itself through you at this very moment.

JEAN HOUSTON

Have a go. When you notice The Thing causing you bother, use your imagination to flip it. Write a new running dialogue in your head to cheer yourself on: *You've got this. You can figure it out.*

STEP ONE

When you keep a writing journal, you find that you can see your obstacles to life more clearly.

Are you standing in your own way?

- Declutter your mean words. The ones stuck on a loop, e.g. *My writing is rubbish, I'm not good enough, I can't do it, I'm not creative.* Grab your journal, and get them down on the page.

- Rewrite any negative beliefs. *My writing is good enough.* Words are powerful. Spin yours into a new writing mantra: *I can do it... I am creative.*

- Get plenty of sleep on inner hygiene days. Think of an inner hygiene day as a reset button.

STEP TWO

PROMPT: Name The Thing.

STEP THREE

PROMPT: Reflect on The Thing; write about it. What does this feeling remind me of from my past?

PROMPT: Write about something as small as a hairbrush, borrowed without permission.

WHAT DOES A WRITER NEED TO KNOW?

He who knows others is wise: he who knows himself is enlightened.

LAO TZU

KNOW YOURSELF

Two thousand years ago Socrates told his students, if you want wisdom Know Yourself. When I finally understood how key it is to Know Yourself in order to be a writer, I panicked and reached for book after book, searching for yet one more expert to explain the riddle of me to myself. I devoured Psychology, Philosophy, Behavioural Science, Neuroscience, Myers-Briggs personality tests, Enneagrams, Archetypes. I even listened to my brother-in-law.

Don't make my mistake. You are the expert on you. Others have no more clarity than you do, they see you through their own sticky lens. You have all your answers inside. Look there. No one is better equipped than you to do this. Self-knowledge is under the clutter in your head.

Try these six questions. They are the questions that we ask our characters, but rarely ask ourselves.

Who are you?

What do you want?

Why do you want it?

How do you do it?

When do you do it?

Where do you do it?

THE KNOW YOURSELF GAME

The more you know yourself, the more patience you
have for what you see in others.

ERIK ERIKSON

Know Yourself tends to focus on the question: Who are you? We often bolt
from this question. Stay with me here. There is a surprising way to answer scary
things.

You have the advantage of being an emerging writer. Be curious. Stay in the
moment. Answer big questions like a small child who announces they want to be
an engine driver when you ask them what they want to be when they grow up.
Play with this game, rather than work hard.

Know Yourself through your heart. Instead of over-thinking, use The Naming
Game to find your answers in your ordinary day. Notice, name and write down
what you discover about yourself.

The trick to doing Know Yourself exercises is do them in microdoses – little
and often. This builds self-awareness, which will makes you a much better
writer.

How do you Know Yourself though the small details of your life?

How do you Know Yourself by what makes you laugh and cry?

How do you Know Yourself when you dissociate from real life or switch off? We learn to disappear into daydreams as a child when we can't fight or flee things that are too overwhelming.

How do you Know Yourself through your good enough side? Kind words, thoughts and deeds?

How do you Know Yourself through what you love? Your friends, your family, your dreams?

Write more about how you know yourself from a small detail in your ordinary life today. Pick one thing. A smile, a slap, an obstacle, your happy place. Set a timer for fifteen minutes and write down the first thing that comes to mind.

STARTER SENTENCE: I noticed this about myself today...

WHY DOES YOUR SHADOW MATTER?

There's a great feeling of relief and catharsis when you manage to get something that's been buried or hidden out onto the page.

KIM ADDONIZIO

———————————

Your 'shadow' is what you don't know about yourself. The shadow is your puppet master – it pulls your strings, but you can't see you are attached to them – when you don't know they are there. You're the last person to spot your own strings.

Psychologist Carl Jung said the first step to knowing yourself is to look at your shadow. This includes all the messy parts of you that society and your family made you believe as a child were unacceptable. You hide these 'unsavoury' bits, and grow up unaware that you have them in your subconscious.

The first step to know yourself is to look at your shadow. Your writing journal is your shield and your sword.

WORKSHOP YOURSELF

How do you rock up in your own life? Are you able to state your anger directly? Or do you act it out? Sulking, outbursts, passive aggression? Can you state your preferences?

Be gentle here. Put out your fires. Don't add fuel to the flames of self-loathing with criticism. A writer is an alchemist. No one knows the power of words better than you. What can you transform that no longer belongs in you?

TIP
It helps to re-name problems as questions seeking solutions.
What if obstacles are opportunities in disguise?

PROMPT: A road trip across inhospitable terrain to meet a secret godmother.

Make a list of things you might want to include in the margin. Set a timer for thirty minutes and write your first draft longhand in one go. Feel your way into this prompt – don't write to impress.

HOW DO YOU KNOW IF YOUR WORK IS ANY GOOD?

When something is important enough, you do it even if the odds are not in your favour.

ELON MUSK

You will never, ever, ever know if your work is any good, not even if you win the Nobel Prize for Literature. And you are not meant to know. A creative person is designed to keep stretching, seeking, evolving. Hilary Mantel said her agent gave her the best advice, early in her career, when she worried if her book idea was good enough. He said, *'Just write as well as you can.'*

Mantel wasted no more time worrying about if her work was any good; she focused on what she could control, she showed up at her desk and she gave writing her best shot.

She writes early in the morning, and doesn't aim for a specific wordcount, but if she can find two hours – in a week – when her writing flows, she has enough for a book.

This gives us all hope we can finish that novel. *'Just write as well as you can.'*

WHAT'S YOUR NEXT STEP?

Writers can get stuck when they don't know what to do next. A little know-how: story craft goes a very, very long way. Think of it as the salt on your food; salt makes your food taste better, but it's not the main meal itself.

HOW DO YOU START TO WRITE A STORY?

If you can't explain it simply, you don't understand it well enough.

ALBERT EINSTEIN

My first writing tutor, the thriller author Sophie McKenzie, taught me a simple way to write a story. Sophie borrowed this from Alfred Hitchcock.

STORY = CHARACTER + OBSTACLE + GOAL

Try C.O.G. before you get bogged down in other more complicated structures, especially if you are a more intuitive writer who is not a fan of plotting. Start with the three C.O.G. questions:

- CHARACTER: *Who* is your character?

- OBSTACLES: What *stops* them getting to their goal too easily?

- GOAL: What does your character *want* or *need* to learn?

Obstacles can be one single thing, but they are usually a blend of these three factors.

- INTERNAL FLAWS: What is your character's internal flaw? Doubt, fear, arrogance, cowardice, unrequited love? Inner hygiene is also useful for this step.

- ANTAGONIST: Who is their opponent? The baddie, wife, boss, children?

- EXTERNAL OBSTACLES: What are their external obstacles? Natural disasters, family, work, society, politics?

TIP: DREAM YOUR STORY INTO BEING

Find three small pebbles; on each, write the initial C or O or G. And then go for what the Japanese call an 'awe walk' – this is when you gaze at everything you see with wonder. Keep the pebbles in your pocket. Turn the pebbles between your fingers and speculate about their story. Dream their story up. Toss the pebbles in the air. Who could C be? What is their goal? What could be their greatest obstacle? Be curious about your story, excited. This is a fun stage. Play.

THE C.O.G. GAME

The character that lasts is an ordinary guy with
some extraordinary qualities.

RAYMOND CHANDLER

Think about a character, their desires, their flaws. What obstacle is getting in the
way of their goal?

EXAMPLE: *Star Wars.*

- The hero is Luke Skywalker; his internal flaw is doubt.

- His goal is to save the rebels.

- His inner need is to find his identity as a Jedi.

- His antagonist is Darth Vader, who is his blood father.

- The external obstacle is a rebellion against the Empire.

Have a go. Break a new story into three steps.

CHARACTER: Who are they?

Set a timer for twelve minutes and write about your character. Or brainstorm a
new one. If all else fails, use a fairy tale set in your home town. The usual sus-
pects to ask about a story are: Who? What? When? How? Where? Why?

CHARACTER PROMPT: Who are you?

GOAL: What does your character want? Or need to learn?

Set a timer for twelve minutes and write about your character's desires and their flaws. Their inner obstacles create conflict and drama for your story. The inner hygiene work you do is invaluable content; fear, grief, doubt, hope are universal emotions. Recycle them into your characters.

OBSTACLES: What gets in a character's way? List your ideas.

Set a timer for twelve minutes and brainstorm the external obstacles and opponents for your character. These obstacles create the conflict and drama in your story.

HOW DO YOU STRUCTURE YOUR BOOK?

I have fallen in love with the imagination. And if you fall in love with the imagination, you understand that it is a free spirit. It will go anywhere and it can do anything.

ALICE WALKER

When I made documentaries about authors, my award-winning TV editor, Barbara Kennedy, gave me the only advice I ever received on structure. A story needs a beginning, a middle and the end.

Really, that was it. Except... Barbara then said that people only remember the beginning and the end. And to put the best stuff there.

This sounds simplistic, and TV is very different from novel-writing, but do master Beginning-Middle-End before you try to learn something more complicated.

In their eagerness to learn more about structure, writers often forget to stick to the basics.

WORKSHOP YOURSELF

What do you think about having a Beginning-Middle-End in every part of your story? How do you think about the Beginning-Middle-End in every scene? Do you think about it in every chapter? In your character's journey? How they change? This too has a Beginning-Middle-End. Do you notice the pattern in your own life?

STRUCTURE: THE STORY RIVER GAME

Writing always seems so private – I can never quite believe that anything I write, especially in longhand, on scraps of paper, which is my usual way of writing, will ever be read by anyone else!

JOYCE CAROL OATES

A simple way to think of story is as a river journey.

Get a big piece of paper, lining paper or a yoga mat. Grab sticky notes, coloured pens. Tape a wiggly piece of string or draw a long wriggly river along the middle of the mat. This is your story line. Do you want it wild or calm? Narrow or immense? Where is it set?

Divide your river into three parts: Act 1, Act 2, Act 3.

Put your main character at the start of their journey on the river.

Put your main character's goal at the end of your river.

Your river needs to flow at different speeds. Boulders/obstacles create this energy. The biggest boulders go on the two vertical lines. These are the end of an Act. Make these obstacles so big your main character can't go back to how they were before.

Put one big boulder in the middle of your river. This is your midpoint. And the midpoint is often a decision that your character has avoided taking, and now they decide to take action.

REMEMBER TO SOAR LIKE AN EAGLE

Stand up and look down at your story river. Imagine you are an eagle soaring over this story. Get your sticky notes and scribble ideas for scenes and obstacles on them. Switch things around until you are happy with the shape of your story river. Think action/reaction for your scenes.

Experiment. Where do you want to put your action/reaction scenes along the river?

Drama is conflict. You need more obstacles and complications in Act 2 to keep the story going.

The final battle – your climax – is near the end of Act 3. What big obstacle could go here?

This is followed immediately by a cool-down – the resolution of your story. It might be a group scene such as a wedding or a dinner so you can tie up the loose ends of all your characters.

THE END.

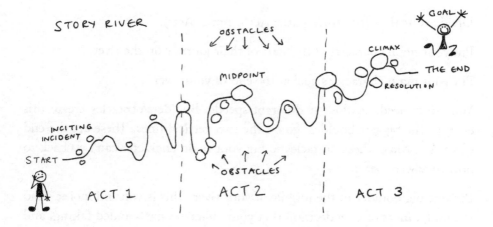

Don't get hung up on story structure. It takes ages to learn. Much of the theory comes from screen craft which is a very different beast from a novel. But the River Structure is a visual, fun, flexible way to see if your story looks balanced before you write.

WHAT DOES 'CHARACTER IS PLOT' MEAN?

Of the many definitions of story, the simplest may be this: It is a piece of writing that makes the reader want to find out what happens next.

BILL BUFORD

The choices that your characters make create your story.

In other words, your plot comes out of your characters' actions and their choices. Structure is not something you have to learn first and then dump your content into it: one size does not fit all.

'Character is plot' is the easiest method for you to write that first draft. It was ages before I grasped this, so don't panic. It feels wriggly, and you don't have to start this way. A story is not some mystifying process that only a few talented writers can pull off.

You already have expert knowledge on how to do this. The emotions that you notice by workshopping yourself in this book can be directly applied to your characters.

Emotion gives your plot energy.
Characters are what give your story emotion.

Your plot is their chain reaction: Action/Reaction. Action/Reaction. When you get stuck, always go back to this foundation: Action/Reaction. Simply ask yourself: now what would my character do? What would they feel about what just happened?

CHARACTERS' CHOICES MAKE THE PLOT

Plot grows out of character. If you focus on who the people in your story are, something is bound to happen.

ANNE LAMOTT

I hope you are feeling empowered, because if you have ever been to a bar with friends, you will be brilliant at asking them how they feel and listening to their stories.

Writing characters requires the same kind of conversation.

You ask characters how they feel. You listen. You watch and see how they respond to an event that just happened. You wonder what action they take next. And you wonder if this new action has consequences. How do they feel now? And so on.

And when your story structure does its job well, no one sees the strings holding it together. This is craft. Imagination made into a physical form. Its shape can be anything, from a song to a novel.

Craftsmen were once apprenticed for *twelve* years in their chosen field. This would give you enough time to respect your tools, and to really know what you are doing.

The next time you beat yourself up for getting stuck: Be kind to yourself. Writing takes time.

WRITING PRACTICE

As for 'Write what you know,' I was regularly told this as a beginner.
I think it's a very good rule and have always obeyed it. I write about
imaginary countries, alien societies on other planets, dragons,
wizards, the Napa Valley in 22002. I know these things.

URSULA LE GUIN

Write a flashback for a character. Set aside a precious writing hour to do this.

OPTIONAL PROMPT: Write a flashback for Goldilocks to show why she
broke into the three bears' home, slept in their beds and ate their porridge.

CHARACTER SKETCH GAME

PROMPT: Invent three new characters. It sounds a lot, right? Look up. What do you see? People.

The secret is to take several people you know and mash them up into one character. Example: Your boss' bad temper, your little sister's pale skin/red hair, and your courageous mother's drinking. The character might be a red-haired alcoholic, courageous and bad-tempered, who plays with dolls.

In seconds you can create a unique, complex character with inner turmoil.

Have a go. Give yourself only fifteen minutes or you will dither.

_____

List three people. What is distinctive about them? Mash them up.

_____

List three more people. What is distinctive about them? Mash them up.

_____

List three more people. What is distinctive about them? Mash them up.

WORKSHOP YOURSELF

What did you notice? What is easy or tricky about creating characters from real people?

Set a timer for thirty minutes. Write about a character's blindness to their flaws and strengths. Or pick a person from your life: what do they fail to notice about themselves?

PROMPT: They never notice...

THE FAIRY TALE GAME

There is the great lesson of 'Beauty and the Beast', that a thing must
be loved before it is loveable.

G. K. CHESTERTON

Write a fairy tale set in your home town. Make a list of ideas. Set a timer for one
hour. I know this sounds like a big exercise, but you just need a rough draft that
will give you material for the next exercises on structure and characters.

PROMPT: If you get stuck, ask these core story questions: Who? What?
When? How? Why?

WHY WRITE IN SCENES?

A scene breaks your book into easily manageable writing chunks. You can decide on the day which scene you are actually going to write. And you can finish a scene in one of your precious writing hours, which will spur you on to write more. Remember the next two tips and you will bypass the common beginner's faults of boring and confusing your reader.

A scene is an event. Something must happen.

A scene unfolds in present time. Something must happen.

- You bore a reader when nothing happens in a scene.

- An event must cause something to change in the scene, or you don't have a story.

- When your scene unfolds in present time, your reader can connect with a character. This is my favourite writing tip. It makes life so much easier.

- This doesn't mean present tense, but writing a scene in present time keeps your imagination in check and reminds you not to add things in that do not belong in the scene.

- When your scene unfolds in present time, you can still use flashbacks. But memories and flashbacks are stronger when they written in present time too.

- Party rules apply to scenes: Make an entrance. Arrive late. Leave early.

An event can be as short as a raised eyebrow. There are no rules for the length of a scene, but it helps to keep them short, at around 1,000–1,500 words. Write one scene a week and you can finish a book in a year.

One warm-up secret is to write content *before the real scene starts* and carry on after it ends. This prevents you freezing. You write about the thing, before The Thing, to get you going.

WRITE A SCENE

All the world's a stage,
And all the men and women merely players;
They have their exits and their entrances;

WILLIAM SHAKESPEARE

Write a scene to show the first time a character appears. How does this character enter the scene?

Set a timer for forty minutes. Keep your opening image strong, simple, and physical. Show The Thing that answers the question: Who is this person? Where are they? Why are they there?

THE KNIFE GAME

If I waited for perfection, I would never write a word.

MARGARET ATWOOD

This is a game to generate ideas, voices and stories for your writing. Play The Knife Game with new friends or family, especially with granny. Secrets and stories come out. Try it in a restaurant waiting for food – but maybe not with your boss – some secrets are hard to put back in the box. Play it with one person or a small group. It's best played fast. I find sugar and wine loosen tongues.

1. Sit in a circle and spin a knife in the middle of the table. When the knife stops spinning, its blade will roughly point at one person to go first.

2. That person has to tell three stories about themselves. Two stories must be truthful.

3. The others guess which one is The Lie. The storyteller must confess which story it is.

4. Then spin the knife again to select another storyteller; rinse and repeat.

5. Take one of these stories and write more about it.

As a writer, this is a fun way to tell and collect stories. You get to practise storytelling and can watch people's faces and see when they lose interest in your tale. You are given the lives of others in highlights. And you get to see what they choose to show about themselves.

EXAMPLE:

Which of these three stories about me is not true?

A: I flew to three European cities aboard Air Force One, and I didn't have my passport on me.

B: A line of school friends played Pass the Pinch at the London Palladium while we sang in a concert, but when The Pinch got to me, I was so ticklish as a young child, I fell off the stage.

C: On my first TV work trip to Asia, I landed in Manila during a military coup. We were surrounded by tanks. I sat atop my suitcase on the runway, next to ITV's Trevor McDonald.

TIPS: SEVEN STORY MANTRAS

These look deceptively simple, but they are very useful to reflect on when you build a story.

1. Life is the choices we make. Plot is the choices our characters make.
2. A character's blindness to their flaws and strengths underpins most fiction.
3. A protagonist is an active character.
4. The stronger their want, the stronger your story.
5. The bigger their obstacles, the better your drama.
6. The more powerful the antagonist, the more powerful your story.
7. Make your characters want something in every scene. Even just a glass of water.

[The answer is B.]

I want to stay close to the groove of people's individual human stories. I can't see that there's anything more interesting than that.

LUCINDA COXON

Take one Knife Game* story and write about it. Why did that person tell you that particular story about themselves? What moments stood out for them in their life? Can you steal it for a story?

---

*The Knife Game is also a game you can play with your characters. Instead of real people, put their names on a bit of paper in a circle, spin the knife and watch the stories pop up in their head. Who do they want to become? And children will tell you stuff about school you didn't know. By the tenth round, they get so excited they barely realise what they are saying. Keep a straight face or they clam up. People get so competitive; you will be intrigued by what you learn about their 'lies'. Listen out for any story that speaks to you and make a note of it for your ideas box.

WHAT DOES 'VOICE' MEAN?

Finding a voice means that you can get your own feeling into your own words and that your words have the feel of you about them.

SEAMUS HEANEY

Your 'voice' is you.

How you speak.

How you think.

And how you feel.

It's your attitude to life.

You need writing confidence to pull off Voice. This comes with practice and self-awareness.

Voice is what you notice and how you put it in your own words. And The Naming Game helps you to naturally connect with your voice by its focus on paying more attention to your life.

Everyone has a different take on Voice. Seamus Heaney put it best and it's worth repeating:

Finding a voice means that you can get your own feeling into your own words and that your words have the feel of you about them.

Heaney believed your natural writing voice is closely connected to your natural speaking voice. The same idea exists in singing – you sing your best when your singing voice is close to your natural speaking voice: push it too high and you will strain your voice and sound false.

There is only one you. You are original by design.

How do think you can get your own feeling into your own words?

THE VOICE GAME

I only know that learning to believe in the power of my own
words has been the most freeing experience of my life. It has
brought me the most light. And isn't that what a poem is?
A lantern glowing in the dark.

ELIZABETH ACEVEDO

STEP ONE:

Learn to appreciate your own voice. Our voices are often lively and engaged
when we talk, but when we come to use our voice for writing we get hung
up on the idea of writing 'properly' and all the energy goes out of our words.
There's a story of a prison whose inmates wrote vivid, funny letters to the
writing tutor, begging for a place on his workshop. But in class, the life went
out of their writing. And nothing the tutor said could persuade the prisoners
to value how they spoke in real life and to use their authentic voices in their
writing.

In *Nomadland* – an Oscar-winning film based on a book about transients
or travellers – the 'actors' were mostly real people, and they couldn't believe
that their voices or their stories mattered. Your voice and your stories matter.
Grab your phone and record your natural speaking voice. Play it back and
listen to it. How do you sound? Do you sound different to the voice you
hear in your head? Does it make you cringe? Or do you like the sound of
your voice?

STEP TWO:

Record your conversations with other people. Just leave your phone on
record, with their permission, as you and your flatmates or your family cook
and eat dinner.

STEP THREE:

Record your voice when you speak to your mother or a sibling on the phone.

STEP FOUR:

Go for a walk and listen to your recordings. Familiarise yourself with how you speak. Be curious, not judgemental. What do you notice?

- Do you interrupt or get interrupted? Do you ever get told to be quiet?

- Do you complain a lot, or nag? Or apologise too much?

- Were you told to be 'good' when you were younger?

WORKSHOP YOURSELF

What did you notice about yourself and your voice from the recordings?

HOW DO YOU FIND YOUR WRITING VOICE?

If there's a book that you want to read, but it hasn't been written yet, then you must write it.

TONI MORRISON

When will you allow your voice to speak? Are you willing to hear yourself? Voice is that simple and that hard to do. Voice happens when you connect to yourself. It's more about listening, being in receiving mode, rather than speaking mode which drowns out guidance. Voice requires space and stillness and knowing what your heart desires.

VOICE IS AN INSIDE JOB

Let's start by how you *don't* find 'voice'. You won't find it by becoming an expert on story craft. If you focus on craft first, you're in danger of becoming slick, with nothing to say. A writing journal is your greatest voice coach. And why you start this book by observing and writing about your life, connecting to how you think and how you feel. This is the first step to finding your writing voice.

The poet Seamus Heaney believed you hear your essential voice in someone else first. You hear something real or read something that thrills you and you wish you'd said it first. And what's happened is you've recognised something essential about yourself and your experience.

Your first steps as a writer will be to imitate consciously, and unconsciously, those you admire. A writing journal is your best friend – you become more aware of what influences you. It feels inauthentic when you add voice as an afterthought to your writing – you try to punch it up but end up speaking like other people and everyone begins to sound the same. For example, too many screenwriters start to say things like 'buckle up' to make their writing sound more thrilling.

Brash is not a better voice – unless it's your true nature – any more than shouting makes for a good conversation. Your voice might be quiet. This voice might be drowned out by noisier others and it's important for you to champion how you speak. Remember that pesky dictum at school – it's better to be a first-rate you than a third-rate Susan. *Be Yourself.* When agents and editors talk about 'voice' they are looking for you to be your own person. And for your story to have its own voice. These qualities come with practice that builds your writing confidence.

THE DIGGING GAME

The first draft is just you telling yourself the story.

TERRY PRATCHETT

Where does your original voice come from? Think way back. Where did your great-grandparents and your grandparents come from? Your grandmother's voice influenced your mother's voice – and hers impacted yours. If your family was fractured, who were the impactors on your voice?

David Almond, author of *Skellig*, says he only found success and his own writing voice when he went back to his Northern roots and described what he saw and heard in his childhood.

Name the places where you lived as a child. How did you feel living there?

What was your original accent?

What did the voices around you sound like?

What institutions moulded your voice? The local football club, Scouts, dance classes, church, school?

Which TV programmes did you watch as a child? Cressida Cowell feels guilty because one of her children speaks with an American accent because he watched so much TV while she wrote *How to Train Your Dragon*.

What music do you love? Martin Luther King used folk rhythms when he wrote his *'I have a dream'* speech.

Do you speak other languages? Each one will have a different rhythm. Isabel Allende says that being multicultural is a huge asset for a writer because it makes you more curious about life.

How many times have you had to adapt your accent? Do you use a particular jargon at work? A lawyer speaks very differently to a builder; both speak differently to their partner than to a colleague.

What did you reject about your original voice?

Example: My original voice was convent-educated-Catholic, Southern-slow-rounded vowels. This got roughed up at art school and changed again at NBC News where they used one swear word – as a verb – for everything. It took me a long time to recognise my voice was influenced by the thing that I had rejected – Catholicism: the rhythm and cadence of prayer. Are there parts of your voice you don't like to acknowledge?

YOUR POWER BOOKS

Picking five favourite books is like picking the five body
parts you'd most like not to lose.

NEIL GAIMAN

Name your favourite books. What stories do you love? List them below.

Reflect on why you love these stories. Set an intention to collect them. Kiran
Millwood Hargrave calls these 'Your power books'. Keep them nearby to inspire
you.

WORKSHOP YOURSELF

Immature poets imitate; mature poets steal; bad poets deface
what they take, and good poets make it into something better,
or at least something different.

T. S. ELIOT

PROMPT: What is The Thing that makes your voice, authentically you?
Set a timer for twenty minutes and write about something that stands out
for you from your past.

HOW DO YOU RUIN YOUR WRITING?

If we only go halfway towards something over
and over, we never arrive.

MEGHAN O'ROURKE

Editing-as-you-go is your hidden time-suck habit; as addictive as smoking, it's incredibly bad for your writing and your mental health. Editing-as-you-go makes you into a learner driver.

Your writing becomes Start-Stop-Stall. At best you will only inch along. At worst, you are trapped in Zeno's Paradox, only going halfway; over and over again. Stuck in repeat mode, you can't finish what you start. And when you polish too early, it's hard to cut it.

Polishing your words as you go makes you feel safe, but it is an illusion. What you are doing is playing mouse, when you need to be an eagle and soar over your first draft.

It makes you doubt yourself, second guess, until you spend all your time over-thinking everything.

IS OVER-THINKING THAT BAD?

Hmm, how can I put this? Over-thinking is worse than over-cooking your food. It spoils everything: the look, the flavour, the smell, the texture, the original shape. And its structure. You get the idea: mushy or burnt and dried-out, over-cooked food tastes bad. Bin it.

But with over-thinking, you believe you can still go back and salvage your story.

You can't.

It's ruined.

You over-cooked it.

I can't bear to tell you how often you see this happen, and how often writers waste more years trying to resuscitate their story. Don't do this. There is a point of no return, when you must either throw the thing away, or start again from scratch, or you must settle for something mediocre.

TIP: FAIL FASTER

Pixar's motto is 'fail faster'. This is to encourage their writers to experiment and take risks. If something doesn't work, the writers bin it and try something else. They don't dwell on mistakes. This helps them to write faster. What can you do to fail faster?

SOAR OVER YOUR FIRST DRAFT

Start before you're ready.

STEVEN PRESSFIELD

The solution is to write a first draft without stopping to edit. A first draft of even one sentence can be so scary that you distract yourself with fiddling. Be brave, it's easier.

Just as you have to let go of the handrail when you ice-skate, you must let go of self-editing when you write. For many of us, jumping into a first draft is daunting. You never feel ready for the ride.

The trick is to not look back. It's exciting, a little bit terrifying, but just get out the front door. Yes, you will make mistakes. Expect them. Trust the process, write. Don't spend weeks overworking something that you have to chuck out later. Just keep going.

Apologies for shovelling on this advice. But I wish someone had drummed it into me. You may not be at the first draft stage of a manuscript yet, but start out as you mean to go on in your writing practice. Master this skill of knocking out your first draft of anything, a poem, even a sentence, without stopping to edit.

And send me a Thank You postcard, because you will be way ahead of everyone.

> **TIP**
> Train yourself to write your first draft without stopping to edit. This soar-like-an-eagle first draft practice will transform how much you can get done.

THE FIRST DRAFT GAME

My own experience is that once a story has been written, one has to cross out the beginning and the end. It is there that we authors do most of our lying.

ANTON CHEKHOV

This exercise shows you what happens when you soar like an eagle over your first draft. The prompt isn't key here; write about anything. The point is to write continuously until the timer goes off. If you get stuck, use The Naming Game practice, just look up and write about where you are.

STEP ONE:

Set a timer for twenty minutes. Write longhand, without stopping.

OPTIONAL PROMPT: What happened to you?

STEP TWO:

Set your timer for another twenty minutes. Now edit and polish what you wrote in the first twenty minutes.

WORKSHOP YOURSELF

What did you notice? I find that I can write three pages longhand in twenty minutes – but I am always shocked to realise I can only edit a couple of sentences in twenty minutes, especially when I began to type up these pages. I sink into mouse mode when I edit. I work on the tiniest thing for ages. Often, in the overall scheme of things, what I polish is not important and gets cut out.

OVERWHELMED? TRY THIS

I have learned over the years that when one's mind is made up, this diminishes fear; knowing what must be done does away with fear.

ROSA PARKS

My bête noir is anything to do with an outline. My mind wants to bolt – I often find that I am halfway out the door before I realise what just happened: my agent asked me for an outline.

Here's what I know now. If you suffer from 'outline overwhelm', it often means the identity of your story is confused. You have too many ideas and you can't decide which ones you love the most. This happens when you don't know what your story is about. Not all ideas belong in the same book, but you can get too attached to them. The result is that you end up with a book that is confused: like fishfingers and curry on your cornflakes. An easy mistake to make when you try to use every craft skill you have ever learned – and every ingredient you have in the cupboard.

THE SOLUTION IS TO WATCH MASTERCHEF

Seriously, MasterChef is a simple, brilliant way to think about story structure and identity. Plus, it looks like you are spending family time on the sofa – when you are thinking about your writing.

The MasterChef contestants make the same two mistakes every week that writers tend to make.

- They add too many ingredients. This confuses the identity of their plate of food.

- And they are asking themselves the wrong question: How can I impress the judges? The finalists always lose when they seek to show off their skills. The solution is always to do less, but to execute your choice of food very well – which only comes with practice and authenticity. Don't show off, show up.

WORKSHOP YOURSELF AS YOU WATCH MASTERCHEF

Every week, the MasterChef judges ask the contestants: What dish are you making?

Ask yourself the same questions as you write.

- What are you making?

- What is the identity of your story?

- When you have too many ingredients, ask: What belongs in this scene/book?

TIPS

When you dream up a new story, come at it through your heart and your body. Send your brain off on holiday and pay attention to the smallest inklings of joy and curiosity.

When you get an idea for a scene, write it down on an index card.

When you have enough cards, about 40–60, divide them into three piles: beginning, middle, end.

What belongs where? Play. This is the most fun stage. Enjoy it. Follow your nose in your first draft.

WHAT IS YOUR STORY ABOUT?

Above all, be the heroine of your life.

NORA EPHRON

This is an exercise to find the identity of your story. Don't worry if you only have a vague idea to start with. Example: My story is about... a Latina single mother... who wants to run for president. Once you have a rough idea of what you want to write about, you can take away anything that doesn't belong in your story of a Latina single mother running for president. Knowing what your story is about helps you to keep your ideas more focused.

Set a timer for twenty minutes, write longhand. Explore. If you get lost, come back to the starter sentence.

STARTER SENTENCE: My story is about...

THE LOGLINE GAME

Thinking is difficult, that's why most people judge.

CARL JUNG

One simple way to structure your book is to write the logline first. The logline is a single sentence that summarises your whole book, shows your theme, your main character and their central conflict. It is fiendishly difficult to write a logline after you have written your book. You will be overwhelmed by the task of capturing your story in one sentence.

But if you start creating a book with your logline already written, you will have such clarity about your story, your logline becomes your compass. And when you write your first draft, anything that does not move your story forward, based on your logline, does not belong in the book.

YOUR LOGLINE IS A COMPASS

First, introduce your character in two or three words. Examples: a visually impaired guitarist, a troubled runaway, a middle-aged footballer. Then suggest their goal/obstacle. Example: the guitarist wants to be a travelling troubadour and walks across America, on her own.

To find your story's emotional core, keep asking yourself: Why do we care about these characters?

If you get stuck, use sticky notes. Move them around on the desk or on a mat on the floor. Try to capture the big picture of your story. Use your new skills; soar like an eagle over this sentence. Do not spend time editing. The most common mistake that writers make is to go mouse and fiddle with the words in a logline rather than simply asking: What is my story really about?

LOGLINE EXERCISE

Don't ever make decisions based on fear. Make decisions based
on hope and possibility. Make decisions based on what should
happen, not what shouldn't.

MICHELLE OBAMA

In the What Is Your Story About? exercise, you wrote about your whole story.
Now tell the core of that idea in one sentence. Keep your sentence to twenty-five
words, or fewer. Example: A female aristocrat falls for an impoverished artist
aboard the ill-fated *Titanic*.

The trick is to write quick, multiple first drafts of your logline and not stop to
polish. Have a go. Set a timer for twenty minutes and write as many versions as
you can.

TRY THIS WHEN YOU FEEL ANXIOUS

Sing something silly. Your writing voice is connected to your natural voice. When you can't get your words out on the page, eventually your voice can get blocked in your throat and becomes energetically stuck in your Throat Chakra.

This energetic blockage travels down to your chest and it feels like anxiety. Almost like panic. You can't catch your breath. It took me ages to understand that my *not writing* was causing this problem.

> **THE CATCH 22**
> You can't write because you feel this anxiety in your chest.
> You feel this anxiety in your chest because you don't write.

DESIGN YOUR ESCAPE POD – WHAT'S THE THING YOU CAN WRITE?

STEP ONE:

Breathe in through your left nostril. Breathe out through your right nostril. Repeat. This calms your brain. Trying humming. Or sing something really silly. And move rhythmically; swaying, dancing, marching around the room. Rhythm helps you to regulate and soothe your body.

STEP TWO:

Set a timer for one minute. Write down a page of anything. Copy lyrics. Scribble a page of gibberish by hand. Just write words. At the same time, tap on your sternum with your other hand; rhythm self-regulates you. Breathe. Then stop. Come back tomorrow.

STEP THREE:

Repeat the process, several times each day. Breathe. Sing. Move. Tap your body. Copy down David Whyte's poem, or a shopping list. Transcribe a recording of your voice. What you write doesn't matter. Just write words on a page and get your writing momentum going again.

Why do this? You are micro-dosing with small repetitive steps – which are in your control. This practice creates new neural pathways in your brain that connect writing with a feeling of safety and familiarity.

Remember the Catch 22. You outwit writer's block only by writing. Once you feel safe, writing, you find that your own words come back, sometimes so swiftly you will be astonished. But start with small, intentional, calm steps. Be gentle, patient and be kind to yourself. And take plenty of rest.

I am too intelligent, too demanding, and too resourceful for anyone
to be able to take charge of me entirely. No one knows me or loves
me completely. I have only myself.

SIMONE DE BEAUVOIR

Gradually, build up your writing practice. Aim to find one precious writing hour,
several times a week, that you protect for yourself.

PROMPT: Write about the moment you find out that your family are in
witness protection.

NO TIME TO WRITE?

This is your life. Do what you love, and do it often.
If you don't like something, change it.

THE HOLSTEE MANIFESTO

You don't have the time not to live your own life. A writing schedule can help get stuff done, but it often feels like another burden on your busy life. It does not address the hidden problems, which are boundaries and expectations. No Time to Write is a boundary issue. This is your life but finding time for you can seem a stretch when everyone is clamouring for your attention. Small tweaks to everybody else's expectations give you the way forward. Be brave. The trick is to do inner hygiene before you draw up a writing schedule.

Make a pie chart of the drains on your time. Where does your time go? Include friends, children, colleagues who gobble your time with their dramas.

Who makes you feel resentful?

OVER-GIVING IS THE CURSE OF 'NICENESS'

How much time is left in your life for writing? Not enough? Over-giving is the yoke of 'niceness' that we strap around our own neck. If you want to write, this has to be removed. Resentment is the clear sign that something is an inappropriate expectation for you. Set a timer for fifteen minutes and write for your life.

WORKSHOP YOURSELF

How were you conditioned to be a 'good' child in your family?

How do you over-give?

Are you always interruptable? Did others learn it is okay to interrupt what is important to you?

THE POEM GAME

Your writing voice is the deepest possible reflection of who you are.
The job of your voice is not to seduce or flatter or make well-shaped
sentences. In your voice, your readers should be able to hear the
contents of your mind, your heart, your soul.

MEG ROSOFF

Write a poem about honour. What does honour mean to you? If the idea of
writing a poem throws you into a tail spin, try this: write your poem first as a paragraph. Put each sentence on a new line. Then edit what you have. Chop it up.
Cut. Cut. Cut. David Bowie generated his highly original song lyrics by chopping
up words from newspapers and randomly mixing them together.

WHEN IT'S NOT WORKING, DO IT DIFFERENTLY

How we spend our days is, of course, how we spend our lives.
What we do with this hour, and that one, is what we are doing.
A schedule defends from chaos and whim. It is a
net for catching days.

ANNIE DILLARD

APPROPRIATE EXPECTATIONS CHECKLIST

Do you have appropriate expectations of what you can get done in a day? Grief, fear, loneliness, work, job loss, home-schooling, elderly parents, exams, illness, rent worries; all kinds of suffering take their toll on you. Take John O'Donohue's advice and shelter in a storm. Rest. Sleep. Reflect. Give yourself permission not to write. Take small steps. Can you adapt the way you write? Short stories, instead of novels? Protect your lunch hour to write one scene?

Fay Weldon wrote in three-line paragraphs; that's all the time she had in between family dramas, with three small children at home.

What can you do differently today?

What can you do differently this week?

TIP
Stop giving advice to others. Save that energy for you. Stop doing their homework. Allow them to grow from their own life lessons.

MAKE A ROTA

Do less. What chores can you delegate to family, children, flatmates and work colleagues? Train them up. It takes time at the start, but it will save your writing in the long-term. Stick with it. Lower your bar on housework and write. Don't volunteer at work, write. This is all easier said than done. Start with One Tiny Thing. Teach children to vacuum. Show them how to work the dishwasher.

Make a rota. Who could do what? When? How?

LOOK AT THE WEEK, RATHER
THAN TRY TO WRITE DAILY

Writing is writing. Writing is not planning or dreaming or talking about writing. When is the best time for you to write? Look at your whole week, aim to find two or three precious writing hours.

How to make this happen? Go to bed earlier, write first thing.

Stop watching TV: save it as your weekend treat. Claw back your time.

Put a schedule on the fridge and protect your precious writing hours like a fierce dragon. Make them non-negotiable. Keep your word to yourself. You promise to write at these times.

WHEN DO YOU PROMISE TO SLEEP?

Sleep is vital for a writer to thrive. You need between eight and nine hours of sleep. And ten hours, like Roger Federer, to recover if you are overworking. I know! None of us sleep enough. And this is why we are all so stressed. Sleep is the only time a clever cerebral writer switches off their thinking brain. You must sleep to recover from stress, overwork and trauma. Your conceptual, frontal cortex cannot repair your body. Stress originates from your older brain; this part of your brain needs to feel safe to stand down. Your inner hygiene practice helps regulate your emotions.

Sleep repairs everything. I'd no idea the harm I was doing to my mind-body by being sleep reckless. Practise self-care. Prioritise your sleep. That said, I am off to bed, two hours late.

REMEMBER TO RECHARGE YOUR BATTERIES

In *The Artist's Way*, Julia Cameron wrote about creative recovery and the importance of taking yourself off on a weekly date with your creativity. The idea is to delight your senses and refuel your spirit. Gift yourself two precious hours alone and go and see anything that is fun and playful, from a museum to a button shop. Notice your own preferences.

TIP: RE-NAME 'OVERWHELM' AS 'ABUNDANCE'

At a buffet, you don't complain all that food is overwhelming. You feel spoiled by its abundance. You know you don't have room to eat everything, so you choose. Turn your writing dilemmas into a pleasure, not a chore. Take your time. Do it bite by bite. Next time you feel confused, pick just one item to do. Try it out. And if it doesn't work, spit it out and pick something else.

WORKSHOP YOURSELF

My mission in life is not merely to survive, but to thrive; and
to do so with some passion, some compassion, some humor,
and some style.

MAYA ANGELOU

There was a lot of craft in Act 2. I wanted to share practical survival writing skills that helped me so you can keep writing when things get tough. How do you feel so far? The mysterious thing about writing is you don't know when you will be ready for a particular tip. Something might not resonate with you at first, but when it does, you step through a doorway and everything looks fresh again. But when something makes you lose focus, that's a sign that it's for another day.

My favourite simple idea is Content is Emotion. Thought is Form. What did you make of that?

How did you get on with C.O.G? Character. Obstacle. Goal.

What was your takeaway from Know Yourself?

More importantly, what have you discovered about your writing? Go back through the workbook and highlight what spoke to you the most. List your insights in the YOUR WORKBOOK HIGHLIGHTS at the back of this book. You've worked hard; it'd be tragic to lose your unique insights. Take the time to capture them. Next time you get stuck, you will have all your best tools in one place.

ACT THREE

THRIVE

IT'S ALL IN THE APPROACH

FOLLOW THE PATH WITH HEART

Follow your bliss and the universe will open doors for
you where there were only walls.

JOSEPH CAMPBELL

In *The Hero's Journey*, Joseph Campbell realised that you can find the path back to you, your life and your creativity when you are brave enough to follow your bliss.

DO WHAT YOU LOVE

Campbell explained when you do what you love, you put yourself on a kind of track that has been there all the while waiting for you. The life you ought to be living is the one you are living.

The focus of this journal has been on noticing your life – the one that you call ordinary, but it's not. In every second, your body makes two million red blood cells. Imagine that.

Everything about you is extraordinary. This time in history is extraordinary. Our souls want us to wake up. How can you do this and follow your bliss? It is so simple; you forget.

GET READY TO BE READY

What sparks your soul is often so small that you don't appreciate it as your first step. We can have a careless approach to life, and discard things that we once treasured, but later forget.

In South Korea when a child reaches their first birthday, older family members place objects on a table – a pencil, a bat, a piece of string, a coin and so on. The elders invite the baby to pick an object.

This one object carries meaning; it is their bliss. Whatever the baby chooses, indicates their soul path. Throughout the child's life, the family remind the child who they are in their heart.

BLISS

What sparks your bliss doesn't matter. It might be unconnected to your writing. But bliss can wake you up. And this alertness wakes up your writing. David Whyte calls it 'getting ready to be ready'.

What is blissful for you could be as simple as warming yourself in the sun.

PROMPT: What is one thing that you once treasured, but you forget to do now?

EXAMPLE:

With one peony, author Rebecca Campbell (no relation to Joseph) found her passion and career. Campbell was a troubled, grief-stricken young person who loved flowers, but realised that she never brought them for herself. She spent her life waiting for someone's else permission to live it.

Campbell made a budget to buy herself flowers once a week. More and more she followed her bliss. She visited parks, photographed gardens. One day she had an urge to post her photos on Instagram. She added fun, rousing words. Fun is the key word here. Campbell was being playful, creative, sharing something she loved with others. Her writing and workshop career took off with a rallying call to other women – *Rise, Sister, Rise*. Her path to bliss started small. With a flower.

HOW DO YOU FOLLOW YOUR BLISS?

If you always do what interests you, at least one person is pleased.

KATHARINE HEPBURN

Start a timer for thirty minutes, and write longhand about one way you can follow your bliss. Take a moment to check-in with yourself. Look for the big picture, something you would love to do, then narrow your focus. Pinpoint what you can do that will take you on that road to bliss. No shoulds, no oughts, the thing you can do. Example: You love colour. What's one thing you can do to bring beauty, the taste of colour into your life? If you get stuck, make a list. Brainstorming gives you a broad focus, then pick one particular thing that you can choose to love more.

STARTER SENTENCE: I love to do…

WAKE UP YOUR SENSES

There is a vitality, a life force, an energy, a quickening that is translated through you into action, and because there is only one you in all time, this expression is unique.

MARTHA GRAHAM

How can you get more bliss into your writing? What can you do to heighten your senses? The more you bring your attention to your senses, the stronger they get.

Heightened attention is called 'flow'. You can train flow by being more present when you do any activity that you love to do and you are good enough at it.

EXAMPLE:

You go surfing on a windy day. Your body is wide awake. It feels like play, but you are hyper-alert. At one with the sea, focused on each wave. You can bring this vitality into your writing.

BECOME THEM: BE THE BAMBOO

Basho, the Japanese haiku poet, taught his poetry students not to merely describe things. Become them, he said. Be the bamboo.

Your senses needed to be fully awake to do this. Playfulness can heighten your five physical senses: sight, sound, taste, smell, touch. You know being in love makes the world seem a brighter place. Colours are more intense. You don't need to wait for love to stir things up; you can do this mindfully. You can make a habit of waking your senses up.

HEIGHTEN YOUR SENSES

You can heighten your sense of sight by imagining, or gazing at something beautiful: your child's face, the sky, a smile. You can heighten your sense of taste when you imagine biting into a peach so ripe that your mouth waters just thinking about it.

TIP

Create your own inspirational playlist for a story or your writing practice. Movie soundtracks, such as Hans Zimmer's music for *Interstellar*, are specifically designed to evoke huge sweeping emotions in the audience. Music is a really quick way to get you in the mood to write.

THE SENSING GAME

Get out of your head and into your body through your senses. You experience bliss through your body. Dial your bliss up. Set a timer for five minutes on repeat.

SIGHT

What is one thing that you love to feast your eyes on? What is one thing you can do to see it more often?

TASTE

What is one thing that you love to taste? What is one thing you can do to taste it more often?

SOUND

What is one thing that you love the sound of? What is one thing you can do to hear it more often?

TOUCH

What is one thing that you love to touch? What is one thing you can do to touch it more often?

SMELL

What is one thing that you love to smell? What is one thing you can do to smell it more often?

WORKSHOP YOUR BLISS

It isn't where you came from, it's where you're going that counts.

ELLA FITZGERALD

What do you notice? Can you feel yourself wake up? How can you bring this sense of aliveness into your story and characters?

EXAMPLE:

If writing an historical novel, you might prepare food in the way your characters might have eaten and celebrate tasting it in a meal with your family or friends. The added bonus is that you build an association with laughter and writing. This makes it easier for you to sit down and write next time. You will associate writing with fun. And you will know the historic taste and texture of this food, which will help anchor your writing.

PROMPT: One thing I can do is…

BE A WILD WISE MAGICAL NATURE CHILD

You are braver than you believe, stronger than you seem,
and smarter than you think.

A. A. MILNE

We all have the 'child archetype'. It lives on in us when we grow up. It is tempting to focus on the 'wounded' child, because suffering is everywhere, but bliss and creativity need a higher vibe.

You can choose to tap into your more joyful child archetypes: the wild child, the nature child, the magical child, the wise child. These are powerful parts of your child psyche that might have met with disapproval in your childhood. Re-awaken these child archetypes and build on the one that feels right for you.

EXAMPLE:

The nature child. This part of you loves wilderness, but you live in a city. How can you re-wild his/her soul? You can't afford to move to the country, so you start small. You might put more greenery on your plate, open your windows at night, take more walks in the park, grow herbs etc.

A LETTER TO ONESELF

Einstein showed that time is not uniform; latest theories suggest the past, present and future are simultaneous. This is a stretch for our logical minds. But, for thousands of years, Buddhist masters have known this. And they had a virtual reality practice similar to our immersive VR games.

Monks would go back into the past, or into the future, and imagine in vivid detail a mentor they admired and whose virtues the monks wanted to process.

This powerful practice is coming back into fashion. Unleash your imagination, visualise and connect to your wise, magnificent inner child.

A LETTER TO ONESELF

We are what we believe we are.

C. S. LEWIS

How to start. Sit quietly. Follow your breath all the way in, all the way out. Close your eyes, slip back to a ten-year-old self. Regardless of how your childhood was in reality, imagine your way to a wild nature child, passionate about life. Set a timer for fifteen minutes and write a letter from them to you. Write fast, as if a teacher is about to snatch your letter away before you can share your secret wish. What do you need for your sparkle to shine? Maybe a tambourine? A sleep out under the stars in the garden? A marble? What does this wild child need from you, to back their dreams?

STARTER SENTENCE: Send me...

WORKSHOP YOURSELF

What did you make of this exercise to tap into your own inner magic?

Practise your own virtual reality. Your brain doesn't know the difference between real and not real. Make regular use of your imagination, creativity, your playfulness or, like any other muscle, they may stop working effectively.

WHAT'S YOUR APPROACH TO LIFE?

I am not afraid of storms for I am learning how to sail my ship.

LOUISA MAY ALCOTT

Survival skills keep you alive. Thriving is all about the way you approach life. The value of a sensitive, wise, compassionate approach holds true for landing an aircraft to how you approach your own writing.

HOW DO YOU SHOW UP BEFORE YOU WRITE?

What is going on in your environment before you start writing? Do you have to get kids off to school or deal with e-mail? Do you write after work? Where do you find peace and quiet to write?

Set a timer for six minutes. Jot down what happens and what you have to do just *before* you write. Do you feel fully prepared, or prefer to wing it? Feel chilled? Or anxious? And procrastinate?

PROMPT: What usually happens…

THE BLANK PAGE

Inaction breeds doubt and fear. Action breeds confidence and
courage. If you want to conquer fear, do not sit home and think
about it. Go out and get busy.

DALE CARNEGIE

Former actor Caroline Goyder gave a TED Talk on speaking with confidence
that went viral. One of her voice coaching tips is from Ewan McGregor.
Before McGregor goes on stage, in his mind, he greets the audience as if they
were old friends. This attitude calms his fear of judgement, his performance
anxiety, and helps his character's voice to sound more natural. This tip is also
very useful for writing.

RELAXED AND CURIOUS

Try this tip yourself. Instead of staring at a blank page (staring is a freeze
response to danger) warmly greet your blank page as your dearest friend. Be
relaxed and curious about what it has to say to you. Talk to it. Blow it a kiss.
Give yourself a hug – this soothes your body while you think. Changing
your approach from fear to friendliness will transform how you feel about
your writing.

GREET YOUR BLANK PAGE

Write a short welcome script to greet your blank page.

TIP: STACK YOUR GOOD HABITS

Attach a new writing habit to something you already do so it becomes automatic. Leave your writing journal by the kettle, or on top of your running shoes, or by your toothbrush. It takes no willpower to brush your teeth. It's a habit. You want a writing practice to be automatic too.

WHAT HELPS YOU THRIVE?

*...it's always possible to find more reasons not
to write a book than to write one.*

MAGGIE O'FARRELL

There are surprising secrets to help you thrive when you write. They come from actors. And neuroscientists.

Actors know how important it is to regulate your emotions before a performance.

They know creativity only thrives when you use your whole body.

Writers believe the myth that you write with your mind. And you often forget that when you sit down to write you are now a performer. You might be giving the performance of your life, and loving what you do, but somehow you can feel stressed at the same time. Neuroscience explains why.

WHEN YOU WRITE, YOUR BRAIN RELEASES STRESS HORMONES

The stress hormones in your brain are called acetylcholine and noradrenaline. Stay with me here, this is super useful – I found it transformative for my writing. Using this knowledge, forewarned, you can prevent writer's block and thrive.

You need the acetylcholine to focus.

Noradrenaline agitates you into taking action.

These stress hormones feel uncomfortable but they are designed to help you. It is easy to misread this as a lack of confidence or a lack of enjoyment in your writing.

Actors know if they go on stage already stressed, performance adrenaline will push them over the edge. Actors take the time to relax first, so this adrenaline feels like excitement.

THE HALF

Actors call this pre-performance time The Half. No actor sprints into the theatre from their outside life, grabs their costume and rushes on stage, still fuming about a late taxi or because small children needed help with their homework. An actor gives themselves half an hour before showtime to unwind. How actors spend this time is highly individual. They might play cards, read a book, do yoga, breathing exercises, or get into character. They tune into their inner self and they dial down their outside life, so they can focus on their performance.

SHOW UP IN THE RIGHT MINDSET

Unwittingly, writers do the opposite. And when you are already stressed, writing can feel like the last thing you want to do. A writing ritual is your secret weapon to show up with the right mindset. Give yourself gentle time to make the transition from your ordinary life to being in the flow.

SET UP AND PAY OFF

Tony Robbins calls this 'priming'. His first hour of the day is dedicated to inspirational reading, a gratitude journal, blessing his family, and a plunge into icy water to toughen his mind and body.

My ritual is similar, but less hardcore. Instead of the plunge I take a dawn walk. I get home, make coffee, take it to my desk and put the cup down as the signal to write. I find the handwritten note for my next step, the kind word or an intention left from yesterday on top of my closed laptop. It's my signpost for that day.

I borrowed this from the television drama *The Queen's Gambit*. When a game is interrupted in a chess tournament, the next move that the player intends to make the following day, gets written down and sealed in an envelope. When the match resumes, the player opens that note and moves their piece accordingly. This same approach takes the dither and wriggle out of writing decisions.

DESIGN YOUR OWN HALF

How could you use the precious thirty minutes to unwind before you write? Write your ideas here.

WORKSHOP YOURSELF

What do you think? Does The Half help your writing? Do you feel calmer or more optimistic when you write? A common mistake is to drop a new habit once it starts working. Hold yourself accountable. Set an intention to do this practice *before* you hit any problems.

WRITING PRACTICE

Repetition is key to your writing success. Keep practising The Naming Game. It will ground you in your life, especially when you are at a time of great change. Look up, what do you see? What particular thing caught your attention today? Set a timer for twenty minutes and write about it. Go back to the Starter Sentence when you get stuck and ask yourself again: I wonder...

STARTER SENTENCE: I wonder...

CHARACTER GAMES

How far would your character go to get The Thing they have always wanted?

Set a timer for twenty minutes and write about this from their point of view.

WHOSE STORY IS IT ANYWAY?

The BBC gets their drama-writing students to ask these questions in every scene in a story. Have a go. Apply these questions to your own story, or workshop your favourite book from memory. Set a timer for thirty minutes, and write longhand.

1   Whose story is it?

2   What does the character need? (What is their flaw? What do they need to learn?)

3   What is the inciting incident? (The disturbance in their ordinary world.)

4   What does the character want?

5 What obstacles are in the character's way?

6 What's at stake?

7 Why should we care?

8 What do they learn?

9 How and why do they learn this?

10 How does the story end?

ARE ANY OF US OKAY?

We live in capitalism, its power seems inescapable – but then, so did the divine right of kings. Any human power can be resisted and changed by human beings. Resistance and change often begin in art and very often in our art, the art of words.

URSULA LE GUIN

No one gets through life unscathed. During the pandemic, a question arose in our global consciousness: *Are any of us okay?* Set a timer for forty minutes, and write longhand for this exercise.

PROMPT: Are any of us okay?

WRITE MOVING CHARACTERS

When writing a novel a writer should create living people; people not characters. A character is a caricature.

ERNEST HEMINGWAY

Readers want to be able to *feel* your characters and be moved by them when they read your story. It is difficult to pull this off. Your best shot at creating empathy, between a reader and your characters, or empathy between characters, is to *feel* their emotions when you write them.

Often, writers come at this from the other end and construct their story like Frankenstein created his monster. Only when they have the body of their novel assembled, characters, themes and structure according to the latest story craft manual, do they try to breathe life into their story. They jump start its heart.

DON'T CONSTRUCT YOUR STORY LIKE FRANKENSTEIN

This kind of over-plotted novel can get up and walk, but not for long. It feels very creaky and dead to your readers, who won't care about the characters. Something is not quite right – instinctively they recognise your characters as not being fully human.

START WITH HEART

The heart is the first cell in a human embryo to develop. Start here in your writing. You are creating something very precious, it's your baby. Care for this small unformed thing, floating about in your head, and give it love as you write it into life. Watch over it, allow it to grow up.

WHAT'S BETTER? A CONCEPTUAL WRITER OR AN INTUITIVE ONE?

No tears in the writer, no tears in the reader. No surprise in the writer, no surprise in the reader.

ROBERT FROST

Neither. We are not binary creatures. Be yourself. Play to your strengths, but also build up your other skills.

Conceptual writers tend to start with form. You smash structure, but you need to connect more with emotion to bring your characters to life.

Intuitive writers feel their way into the story and often start with character. Everyone loves your characters, your beautiful writing, but they get lost and give up reading, confused by your story.

The rule of thumb is intuitive writers fare best when they start with a smidgen of structure and ask themselves: What is the main thing I am trying to say here?

And conceptual writers do best when they start with character and hold off on plot.

WORKSHOP YOUSELF

As a writer, which matters more to you: thought or emotion? Where do you put your attention? How you answer this question will tell you about the kind of writer you are.

PROMPT: A mother drops a running-away bag out of her bedroom window. Set a timer for a precious writing hour and write a scene, story or a poem about someone desperate to escape their life.

WHAT CREATES HEART IN A STORY.

Be sure not to discuss your hero's state of
mind. Make it clear from his actions.

ANTON CHEKHOV

———————————

The secret is to create empathy with your reader. How do you do that? Take a moment to consider what you do in real life to get understanding and sympathy from your friends. You tell them a story, and you tend to exaggerate what feels unfair or sad or unlucky. People empathise, because they can identify with your pain and suffering, as these emotions are universal.

Pixar's writers are *the* experts when it comes to emotional storytelling. It is worth having a look at what they do. Empathy is Pixar's signature skill. Pixar have a formula to help their writers create emotional, fully-rounded characters that the audience will love. It runs as follows:

$$EC = EM (R+P^2 + H+A+ ES + (MS))$$

Don't panic; it's easier than it looks. By the end, you'll be able to sleepwalk your way through this.

STEP ONE: Find the Emotional Core of your story.

STEP TWO: Create Empathy between your characters and your audience.

STEP THREE: Use Recognition, Pity, Human, Admiration, Emotional Stakes + Meaning.

E SPECIFIC YOUR STORY, THE MORE UNIVERSAL ITS APPEAL

eate empathy and your readers will love your characters. Empathy is more powerful, more subtle than merely making your characters likeable. You can have a social misfit like Eleanor in Gail Honeyman's award-wining debut novel *Eleanor Oliphant Is Completely Fine* but you love and empathise with this character because we understand Eleanor.

Is your head spinning? Mine was. It is a lot to take in, but it's really useful. Pixar suggest six things for you to think about that will help to make your story the best it can be.

RECOGNITION

Your readers recognise their own emotions in your character. Love, fear, hate, envy, joy, embarrassment and hope are universal emotions. The trick is to show universal emotions in a specific context. The more specific your story, the more universal its appeal. It feels counter intuitive, doesn't it? It took me ages to get my head round it. But you have the advantage: everything in your writing journal is about being specific, about looking up and recognising things by name.

Have a go. Set a timer for six minutes. Write about something that embarrasses you. Focus on an emotion in a specific context.

PITY

People empathise with an underdog. The more unfair and cruel a situation, the more you root for the character. Pixar consider pity so important the P^2 in their formula reminds writers to load on painful, unfair obstacles to make us care. That's why Harry Potter lived under the stairs, with a cruel uncle and aunt – we were on his side from the outset.

Have a go. Set a timer for six minutes. What are the unfairest things that have happened to you? Bring that authenticity to your writing.

HUMAN

Your reader must be able to see your characters as one of us. Even if you write sci-fi or historical figures, or create monsters and baddies. Example: Pixar's WALL-E. He is shown as the lonely trash-collector, a robot yearning for love and connection, watching old romantic movies. We can all relate to that.

Writers show superhero characters as human. In *The Incredibles*, Elastigirl (Mrs Incredible) sulks as she vacuums. She resents cleaning the house. We recognise that feeling of injustice that we all have when you do more than your fair share of the chores.

Have a go. What can make your character seem more human? Hollywood uses Save The Cat. If a character feeds their pet once, the audience assumes they're a good person and likes them. Set a timer for six minutes.

ADMIRATION

Humans like to admire people. Superhero stories max out on this idea. The skill in writing comes when you can create empathy with smaller admirable acts of bravery or kindness. What is one core talent or quality that you can *show* your protagonist has, for readers to admire?

EMOTIONAL STAKES

What is at stake in your story? The trick is to set your character's stakes really high. When their world doesn't change in some way and it doesn't matter if they fail or not, then you don't have a strong enough story.

Have a go. What happens if your character fails to reach their goal? Set a timer for six minutes. Imagine a goal and ask yourself, what are the stakes?

MEANING: THE WHY OF YOUR STORY

Why does your character care about their particular goal? Your story goal doesn't have to be life and death, it could be about a character coming to terms with loss; but it must matter to them. They must care and you must know why they want it or the reader won't care if they get there.

Have a go. This is tricky, so take your time. Write about something you care about and then bring that emotion in your story.

TIP
You don't need equal amounts of salt to meat in your dish. Go easy on story craft. Don't use everything at the same time. Or in equal amounts. Some things matter more than others. Use story craft to help you think about your writing, not to cause mayhem and overwhelm you.

INSTANT RELAXATION TIP

It takes a great deal of bravery to stand up to our enemies,
but even more to stand up to our friends.

J. K. ROWLING

Neuroscience says when you want to feel calmer, let your eyes go panoramic.

This means being wide-eyed instead of focusing on one thing.

Humans are prey animals – when you go wide-eyed you send a message to your brain to stand down and relax. We do this naturally when we look up at the sky or at a horizon.

In life drawing, artists 'un-focus' their eyes to widen their view and get an overall impression of their subject. This saves them from getting too bogged down in detail when they draw.

This approach is incredibly useful for writers too, especially when we stare at a screen all day. We are generally unaware how much this short-range focus on a computer is stressful for the mind and body.

TIP
Set a timer on repeat for every hour and build a habit to look up from your work and glance out of the window. It takes a moment. Try it now. Go and look out of a window. Look up.
Can you feel your body relax when you exhale and let your eyes go panoramic?

Don't trust the right thing done for the wrong reason.
The why of the thing, that's the foundation.

JONATHAN NOLAN

Write about a father trying to get back home to his daughter. What is his core emotion? Longing? Desperation? Hope? Determination? Where will you set this scene? In space, like *Interstellar*? Or a dad stuck at work who wants to be at his child's birthday? Set a timer for thirty minutes. Have a go. You are after the embryo – a tiny seed of an idea – not a finished piece.

FIND YOUR HEART GAME

What quality do you most admire in a person and might want to explore in a story? Come at this from your heart, not just your thinking mind. Start by brainstorming an empathy list. Muck around. And take plenty of breaks.

What core value do you most admire?

Honesty, bravery, love, hope, truth, compassion, confidence.

_____

What professions/situations best test/show this quality?

_____

What goal would best test this quality?

Why do they want it? Think about the reasons why your character wants their goal.

___

How can you best show the character arc of this quality?

Think how you might start. What happens if you start with its opposite value? EXAMPLE: A cowardly firefighter must learn to be brave.

___

What environment and setting could best show this quality?

EVOKE YOUR CHARACTER

Writing is a process, a journey into memory and the soul.

ISABEL ALLENDE

A character interview is a powerful process that actors use to prepare for a role. The actor asks themselves questions as if they were the character. The trick to is to see your character as a real person and ask them the same things that you might ask a friend, e.g. What do you eat for supper? Where did you hide the body? And write down the answer that pops into your head.

Set a timer for thirty minutes. Close your eyes, take a few deep breaths to ground yourself first, then imagine your character sitting opposite you, and start to talk to them.

PROMPT: Tell me, what do you really care about?

GO FOR A WALK AS YOUR CHARACTER

Writing is a job, a talent, but it's also the place to go in your head. It is the imaginary friend you drink your tea with in the afternoon.

ANN PATCHETT

One simple way to find your character is to go for a walk as them. Many authors shrug on their fictional overcoat in the same way an actor takes on their new identity in a role. Costume helps an actor bring their role to life. It's the same for a writer. Play make-believe. Dress up. Wear a similar coat or boots to a character. Go out unkept, if they live rough. Walk with their physicality and their attitude to life. When they see a smart car, do they resent, covet or admire it? Where do these feelings you imagine show up in your body? Use The Naming Game to find the words for them.

Chat to your character. Ask them, What do you want to do in the story next? Then let it go. Chill, and just walk. Make a note of any flashes of insight as they happen, and then write more at home.

STARTER SENTENCE: On my walk, my character feels…

THE SKILLS GAME

What talents do you secretly wish you had? What skills do you wish you had learned or would love to have? Make a bucket list of Dream Skills. Go wild, anything from a beetle expert to a sushi chef to an intergalactic geologist. Set a timer for thirty minutes and dream up twenty-five things you would love to do or know about.

1

2

3

4

5

6

7

8

9

10

11

12

13

14

15

16

17

18

19

20

21

22

23

24

25

INVENTION GAME

You'll need a new notebook, colourful index or playing cards, three pebbles, and a marker pen. Ring six to eight talents or skills off your list. Write them down on the back of the playing/index cards, or bits of torn paper. Shuffle and deal these skills cards to an imaginary person in front of you.

What is the most exciting, unlikely combination? Pick three things.

Set a timer. Do one hour of research on these skills. Give specific details.

Drill down further. What excites you about them? Can you take a class in one of these skills? Talk to an expert in this field? Ask them for their stories?

- What kind of character could have these skills?

- Set a timer for four minutes. Dream up a character you'd love to have in a story.

- Set a timer for ten minutes. Where could this story belong? (What place would you love to visit/research for a story?)

This is the fun bit. Muse on the possibilities.

- Who belongs in this story?

- Write on three pebbles: a name, a skill, a place.

- Keep these pebbles in your coat pocket and rub them together with your fingers when you go out for your writing walks. Throw the pebbles up in the air and imagine the story world around them. Wake up this story. Call it to you.

EMOTIONS PRECEDE THOUGHT

In a very real sense we have two minds, one
that thinks and one that feels.

DANIEL GOLEMAN

People can rarely name their emotions; they act them out. As a writer you need to be able to capture how people show their feelings. The same skills that you use in The Naming Game can help you become more emotionally intelligent.

We tend to be either a more intuitive writer or a more conceptual one depending on our strengths. The internationally renowned psychologist Daniel Goleman champions emotional intelligence over intellectual ability. Anyone can learn this skill. There are four elements:

1. self-awareness

2. self-compassion

3. self-mastery

4. empathy.

TIPS: EMPATHY
There are three different types of empathy; this knowledge is a useful writing tool.
- Cognitive empathy is understanding how people think and act.
- Emotional empathy is understanding how they feel.
- Compassionate empathy – this is the big one – this is really *caring* about how they feel and think, as a parent cares for a child.

WHAT EXCITES YOU ABOUT WRITING?

This is probably the most important thing for a writer to know about themselves. What excites you the most about writing? Do you love words? Stories? Puzzles? Emotional content? What's your thing? Set a timer for twelve minutes. Shoot from the heart, letting loose your arrows of desire.

STARTER SENTENCE: What excites me most about writing is this... and this... and this...

I LOST MY MOJO: WHAT CAN I DO?

There is more wisdom in your body than in your deepest philosophy.

FRIEDRICH NIETZSCHE

Gratitude is the cure for this. When you practise daily appreciation for the little things that life brings you, no matter how small, your joy in living and writing returns. Run some cool water over your wrists, and imagine it's the first clean water you've seen in a month.

Add a Gratitude Practice to your writing journal. Gratitude journals are all the rage; every successful soul, from Oprah to Matthew McConaughey, keeps one. Take a moment every evening, before you go to sleep, to draw your attention to something you appreciate about your writing. Maybe you read a great line in a book. Or you are grateful that you have your eyesight. Or you have a dream to be a writer.

I am grateful for…

This joyful thing happened today…

I might do this differently…

NEUROSCIENCE FOR WRITING CONFIDENCE

BREATHE TO THRIVE

Did you notice that you got more stressed when you worked exclusively on screens at home during lockdown?

Your breathing can relax or stress your body. Writers unwittingly have a bad habit. We hold our breath when we work on a screen. It's called 'e-mail apnoea'. And 80% of us do it.

This unconscious habit makes your body feel very anxious. Holding your breath is a freeze response to danger. Back in the day when we saw a predator, we focused on them, and held our breath so they wouldn't hear us. Your brain doesn't realise that focusing on a screen isn't life or death, but the focal length between the screen and your eyes will still stress your body.

Here is a neuroscience trick to regulate your body. Slow your breath down and inhale/exhale through your nose. Try this now. Set a timer for one minute. Take a slow breath in and out through your nose. See if you can slow your breath to about eight–ten breaths a minute. What did you notice? How much calmer do you feel?

SIT UP TO THRIVE

Sit up straight when you write and relax your shoulders. This is a HUGE tip. You will feel much less anxious. Your posture affects your breath. You can't write your best if you slump at your laptop. Your writing voice, your writing confidence, are intimately connected to your breath.

TRY THIS:

Take a writing break. Relax your shoulders. Put your hands on your diaphragm. Take a deep breath in through your nose, so you feel your ribs move. Let it go. What do you notice?

LOOK TO THRIVE

Your eyes are the only parts of your brain outside your skull. Your eyes help regulate anxiety. When your eyes focus on a screen, your brain releases acetylcholine, which makes you feel agitated. After writing, don't immediately stare at your phone. It's the same focal length and still stresses your mind. The trick is to glance up at the sky or the horizon – and let your eyes go *panoramic*.

TRY THIS:

Stand up and walk across the room – look out of the window. Take a breath. What do you notice when your eyes look at the sky? Can you sense you feel calmer? You have been using this trick in The Naming Game practices. Do it now. Look up, what do you see? Write.

WALK TO THRIVE

Every time you take a step, your eyes move laterally and tell your brain that your body is out of harm's way.

Walking tells your brain to stand down. The brain knows your body is moving from your eye movements, not your limbs. This is why writers feel relaxed when they walk.

And an early morning walk improves sleep because the light resets your circadian rhythm to sleep sixteen hours later. This trick alone cured my insomnia.

TRY THIS:

Grab your keys and take a quick awe walk. Look up at the sky. Slow your breath, then come back after a few minutes.

WORKSHOP YOURSELF

How do you feel? Our culture loves people who push through and keep going when stressed. But it is counterproductive in the long term, especially for a writer. Your thinking brain can't fix stress. Only sleep, and relaxing your body by using your eyes and breath, can tell your mind to stand down.

YOUR INNER GUIDANCE

Mystical guidance enters you softly, like a thought that suddenly occurs to you out of the blue. I learned to take notice of that 'sudden, out of nowhere' sensation.

CAROLINE MYSS

Did you skip the WORKSHOP YOURSELF pages? You might feel you know the answers in your head, but there will be stuff hiding under the surface. You need to invite it into the open so you can crack on with your writing.

TRY THIS:

Set an intention before you workshop your writing. The way to do this is to ask your writing journal questions:

- How can you get one great idea for a novel?

- What can I do today that will inspire me to write more?

- What is a good name for my character?

- I wonder how my story will end?

- What do you want to say?

- How can you say it better?

These questions will prompt your own answers. Then be still. Listen to the magic happen.

Doorways unlock inside you. Unexpected guests show up to the party. It takes time to recognise their gifts and put a name to their faces. Insight. Synchronicity. Ideas. A-ha moments rock up.

SCEPTICAL?

Me too. I was a total sceptic about this. I didn't journal – until 2020. And then I had my best year ever – during a pandemic. This practice of being mindful, intentional about your writing is transformational. I'd no idea what was going on, until I realised that asking questions is an invitation to accept invisible help. The Law of Ask and You Will Receive really works.

But the catch seems to be that you get what you *need* to grow – which is not at all the same thing as what you *think* you *want* to receive.

Trying to control the outcome is often why you often don't realise you've been given your answer.

EXAMPLE:

I asked *How do I structure my book?* I wanted a download of the outline. A roadmap. But what I got were flashes of the sections I needed to assemble – I realise now that all I had to do was put them in the right place in the jigsaw at the time I got them – one by one.

I'm dyslexic, good on spatial thinking, and this would have been easy for me. I was prompted to construct the book like a theatre nurse anticipates the needs of the surgeon, by handing them the right surgical instrument in the right order before they ask. But I put the tools I was given aside, ungrateful, complaining I still didn't have a clear outline. I missed my answer; I was expecting something else. It's a subtle process listening to your intuition. Your way, and your challenges, will be different to mine – an outline for an editor would be a breeze: writing a novel not so much.

Trust me. Go back. Use every WORKSHOP YOURSELF feature in this journal. Listen to how your own questions prompt answers. A writing journal clears out the clutter in your head to make space for you to hear your intuition. Your job is to take action on it. A good question is more powerful than the answer. And some questions are so big, you need to repeat them before you hear an answer. Plant the seeds in your own mind.

TIP
Re-name doubt as curiosity.

CATCH YOUR OWN FISH

Give a man a fish, and you feed him for a day.
Teach a man to fish, and you feed him for a lifetime.

CHINESE PROVERB

Writing prompts have their place, but it is much better for you to teach yourself to catch your own fish. Start close in. Who did you see today? What small thing happened today? What's the most unlikely combination you think of to mix things up?

Have a go. Set a timer. Make up twelve writing prompts in six minutes.

1

2

3

4

5

6

7

8

9

10

11

12

FUTURE AUTHOR AWE WALK

One of the hardest things for an emerging writer to do is to claim their rightful place in the world. Writers suffer from Imposter Syndrome. You feel too self-conscious to admit your writing dream when you haven't finished your first book or short story. Train yourself to confess that you are a writer when people ask you who you are: not what job or role you do. Share your passion.

Imagine yourself at your first Writers Anonymous Meeting – you must find the nerve to stand up and say, I AM A WRITER.

Grab your keys and go for a walk as this writer. Imagine the confidence of your future author in your body. Feel your skin tingle with excitement.

YOU ARE THE WRITER

You need support to be a writer. It helps to find your tribe. Start small. Can you reach out to a writer in an online group? Start your own group from this workbook? Find a mentor? Take a class? What can you do to find your tribe to support you?

WORKSHOP YOURSELF

How do you feel? What is one thing that changed for you by using this workbook?

Your writing voice is the deepest possible reflection of who you are. The job of your voice is not to seduce or flatter or make well-shaped sentences. In your voice, your readers should be able to hear the contents of your mind, your heart, your soul.

MEG ROSOFF

What really matters to you? Family, love, success, growth, friends, discernment, survival, expressing your creativity? Sense the answer in your body. Set a timer for twenty minutes, don't stop until it goes off – keep going back to the starter sentence.

STARTER SENTENCE: This really matters to me...

THE WHAT IF? GAME

Asking *What if?* questions prompt you to re-imagine other people's lives and stories without getting too sidetracked by research.

Asking *What If?* is how many authors, such as Stephen King, generate their story ideas. It throws up creative situations and new contexts for you to explore in a story.

EXAMPLES:

What if Henry VIII had lived on a council estate?

What if Henry were short for Henrietta?

What if Henrietta had six different husbands in six different galaxies?

What if she had to pick just one life?

See how your mind plays with these ideas? And repetition generates more ideas. Have a go.

WRITING PRACTICE

Take a celebrity or newspaper story and switch it up – put a famous person in a different context. First, stand up and do ten star jumps to pump up your energy. Put your timer on repeat for one-minute sprints. Aim to do ten silly, diverse, dangerous *What ifs?*

What if…

What if…

What if…

What if…

What if…

What if…

What if…

What if…

What if…

What if…

THE *WHAT IF?* CHALLENGE

Aim to do at least one *What if?* a day for a month.

Get in the habit of generating ideas.

Brainstorm *What ifs?* with friends over a drink, or with the kids – use a timer – and see how many they can do in ninety seconds. There's nothing like a deadline to make them competitive.

Keep a list. Mix and match ideas. See if anything grabs your interest, follow it up and write some more.

Step into your writing with childlike curiosity. A writer chooses to expresses their creativity though their love of words and story and we assume that this means we start with learning to write. But a better place to start is with your creativity. Allow your writing to breathe like a fine wine. Create space around it. Throw ideas up like juggling balls. Create space in you to catch them

----

WORKSHOP YOURSELF

If you could do one thing in your writing, what would it be?

You must write. It's not enough to start by
thinking. You become a writer by writing.

R. K. NARAYAN

PROMPT: Write about a character who finds the space to breathe in
their life.

THE BOOK COVER GAME

You were the miracle you didn't believe in.

ROBERT BRAULT

Sometimes, you need a bit of magic to fire you on and keep believing in that novel or short story. Bestselling author Wayne Dyer always imagined his Work-In-Progress as a real thing before he actually wrote it. He would print off the title with his name underneath and wrap this mock cover around another book. This was his message to the universe, an intention to write this book.

When I road-tested this tip, I was astonished at how powerful it feels when you actually wrap your mock cover around another book. It feels very different from just printing it off. Have a go.

STEP ONE:

Find free book cover design software. Canva is the best one that I know. Don't worry too much about your title – publishers often change that anyway. A good working title often just says what your story is about. *No Boy is Worth Your Soul* was the idea in my head when I wrote my Young Adult book *The Hurting*. And its original title was *Hurts So Good*.

My title is:

STEP TWO:

Mess around with Canva. Design your own beautiful book cover. Get creative.

Canva is very simple to use and a lot of fun. Allow your mind to play. Experiment with colour, shape and images. What setting and atmosphere do you want? What styles do you like? Nordic Noir, lyrical, minimalist, traditional? Pour imagination into this dream book.

Add the book title and your name to the spine of your book.

Write endorsements from your favourite authors for the back of your book. This is something you do on an MA Publishing Model. I used Michelle Paver and Lee Child on the back of my novel.

My author endorsement(s):

Write your book blurb. Keep it simple, just a few lines about your story.

PROMPT: My story is about…

STEP THREE:

Print off your cover and wrap it around one of your own 'power books'. Choose an author you admire – and let their magic animate your book. My mock-up cover for this book was wrapped around John O'Donohue's poetry. As silly as this sounds, this is a secret power game. It feels thrilling. You can believe your book is really going to happen. One well-known author takes herself off to a local bookshop and puts her finger on the shelf where her book would go. It inspires her to keep going. Where does your book belong in the world? Your book is no longer this abstract thing in your head. It is now a physical object on your desk calling you to do the work.

WORKSHOP YOURSELF

How did this task help to focus your story? Did it inspire you to write?

TELL THE STORY OF HUMANITY

You must not lose faith in humanity. Humanity is an ocean; if a few drops of the ocean are dirty, the ocean does not become dirty.

MAHATMA GANDHI

How did you feel when you read the title of this exercise? Did it throw you into a tailspin? How can you break it down into something smaller and more manageable?

What if you just show a golden couple risk everything for something that was forbidden to them?

This is the story of Adam and Eve. This is the story of humanity. Greed. We were given the Earth, but wanted more, and we threw away the most precious thing we had. Can you rewrite this story?

What if you wrote humanity's story as the caretaker/guardian story? Show a character who wants to care and share? What would be their obstacle? Temptation? Where would you set this? When? Why? Set a timer for thirty minutes. When a task seems this vast, come at it from the perspective of a wise, unselfconscious child who just writes it down in the sand and retells their story around a campfire.

STARTER SENTENCE: My story of humanity is…

RITUAL

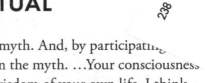

A ritual is the enactment of a myth. And, by participating
ritual, you are participating in the myth. ...Your consciousness
is being re-minded of the wisdom of your own life. I think
ritual is terribly important.

JOSEPH CAMPBELL

Ritual brings a sense of the sacred into your day; even if you don't think
of yourself as spiritual, it transforms routine into creative magic. The Half
calms your mind and body before you write; your ritual connects you to your
heart and soul. A musician might play Bach every morning, you might go for
a walk, or bless your family. According to Ashley River Brant in *Tending to
the Sacred*, your ritual needs four things:

- intention

- trust

- heart

- space.

INTENTION

You will transform your day and your writing if you set an intention to connect with the sacred before you write. Say a prayer, send a blessing, ask for
guidance. You can do this in a heartbeat; you don't need to be earnest, your
soul loves joy. Play music. Dance, sing your intention into being.

TRUST

Trust is sacred listening. A belief that something listens back. This might be a stretch for you. I find walking works wonders for me; I set an intention for guidance and trust that an answer will come. It does, but not how I expect. The trick to is to act *as if* something listens back until you know what to do next.

HEART

The way to love is to give your full attention, whether it's to a novel or a child. Pour love and attention into your writing ritual. Your heart is the way to your soul. Imagine it wide open and full of love.

SPACE

Create an inviting space around your ritual that welcomes in the sacred. Treat your space with respect. It might be as simple as decluttering, lighting a candle or putting a flower on your desk.

DESIGN YOUR OWN RITUAL

How can you bring a ritual into your every day? Anything can be a ritual. For choreographer Twyla Tharp, her morning ritual is making a 05.00 call to her cab company to take her to the gym – her personal sacred space. After that phone call, everything falls into place for her daily practice. Have a go. Start small. Think of one thing you can do for each of the four elements.

Intention: What intention could you set for the day?

_____

Trust: What can you do to practise sacred listening? A breath, a prayer, a meditation?

_____

Heart: What can you do to love and pay attention to yourself?

_____

Space: What one thing can you do to create a more inviting space in your life?

COURAGE

To speak one's mind by telling all one's heart.

The word 'courage' originally meant to speak your mind by telling all that was in your heart. How beautiful is that? What would you write about if you had the courage to write it? What would scare you the most to write about? Ground yourself with a few slow breaths. Set a timer and give yourself eight minutes to write what is in your heart. The trick with this kind of prompt is to dive right in and write down what comes to mind.

STARTER SENTENCE: If I had the courage, I'd write about…

IT'S A WONDERFUL LIFE GAME

To see that your life is a story while you're in the middle of living it
may be a help to living it well.

URSULA LE GUIN

It's A Wonderful Life was based on a book: *The Gift*. A family man wants to jump from a bridge when he thinks his life is a failure. As in Dickens' *A Christmas Carol*, the story asks *What if* you were given a Life Review? What if you were shown how every tiny act of kindness you performed touched the lives of others? Life has been hard these past few years, and there's a market for uplifting stories. What's yours?

Have a go. Set a timer for twenty minutes and write about how one small thing, maybe a kind smile or word, at the right time, changed your life.

THE MUSE GAME

I gift you with the courage to be, to know deeply the divine design of your life. I gift you with passion for the possible and the willingness to bring this possibility into time. You are more than you think you are, and something in you knows it.

JEAN HOUSTON

Set a timer for sixty minutes: Write the lyrics for the song you secretly want played when you go out to save the day.

Tell me, what is it you plan to do with
your one wild and precious life?

MARY OLIVER

How would you approach Mary Oliver's beautiful question? Take a few breaths. Then make an intention to consider your one wild and precious life with wonder. Set a timer for twenty minutes, and write stream of consciousness. Come back to the starter sentence if you get stuck.

STARTER SENTENCE: Tell me, what is it you plan to do with your one wild and precious life?

Do this exercise once a month. It gives you a north star for your life and for your writing. This is a Soul Question. You won't find a way to answer it though your intellect. The way is through your heart. And it will take you a lifetime to come close to answering it. The trick is to take the time to enjoy it. Sift your insights, like fine sand, and savour them one grain at a time.

YOUR WRITING JOURNEY

Forever is composed of nows.

EMILY DICKINSON

The strangest thing happened to me when I researched this commission for *Writers' & Artists'*. Another book wrote itself; *A Writer's Soul Journey*. At the time, I was road-testing new writing exercises and found that everything I was asking about my own life and my writing was answered.

On long dawn walks, through insights, synchronicities and guidance, I discovered what I believed; about the Universe, God, what my life means, and its purpose. I shared this transformation in a daily, year-long conversation with my school friend, Sally Thirkettle. I had walked into my real life. A sense of joy flowed into all parts of my life. I was keen and curious and joyful to explore my own writing again. As you still are, I hope.

But I also know that you are in great peril of replacing this joy with crazy levels of doubt and fear and anxiety later on. This self-doubt plagues writers. My intention was to find a way for you to avoid these pitfalls and thrive. I spent time wondering why some writers start out happy at the start of their writing journey, but so many seem tortured by the end.

The answer came to me that the Child is the metaphor for a Beginner's Mind. And the catch is the more you learn, the more the writer in you becomes a Grown-Up. This writer demands grown-up things like money and significance to show for all your hard work. Understandable. You are a storyteller at heart, and since the dawn of time, storytellers have passed on their musings and wisdom to others in the form of stories. Storytellers need an audience. But in your rush to find one, the stress rubs out the excitement of your writing, and fun, and endless, magical possibilities.

So often, when you go to a writing workshop, what you learn stays in the classroom. If you take anything from this workbook, use a writing journal to workshop yourself. Protect your curiosity, your sense of adventure. Trust yourself. Write with self-compassion. Love your writing, no strings attached. And be careful what you wish for; don't grow up too fast. Slow down, enjoy the ride.

What is one thing you can write today? A scene? One sentence? The first page of your book? Look up, what do you see? This is your life; and it needs you. Grab a pen. *Write. Write. Write.*

YOUR WORKBOOK HIGHLIGHTS

YOUR OWN INSIGHTS

What spoke to you in this workbook? What insights, ideas, rituals came to you? Don't lose your self-knowledge. Go back and capture it. List it here. I wish I had kept all my tools in one place. And take a bow. This has been intense, and you are still here. What will you write next?

YOUR OWN INSIGHTS

YOUR OWN INSIGHTS

RESOURCES

Less is more. Here are a few books, sites and experts to inspire you.

Julia Cameron, *The Artist's Way: A Spiritual Path to Higher Creativity*
Anton Chekhov, *Short Stories*
John O'Donohue, *Divine Beauty: The Invisible Embrace and Anam Cara: Spiritual Wisdom from The Celtic World*
Clarissa Pinkola Estés, *Women Who Run With The Wolves: Contacting the Power of the Wild Woman*
Elizabeth Gilbert, *Big Magic: How to Live a Creative Life, and Let Go of Your Fear*
Natalie Goldberg, *Writing Down the Bones: Freeing the Writer Within*
Caroline Goyder, *Gravitas: Communicate with Confidence, Influence and Authority*
Gary Keller, *The ONE Thing: The Surprisingly Simple Truth Behind Extraordinary Results*
Stephen King, *On Writing: A Memoir of the Craft*
Annie Lamott, *Bird by Bird: Instructions on Writing and Life*
Jorjeana Marie, *Improv for Writers: 10 Secrets to Help Novelists and Screenwriters Bypass Writer's Block and Generate Infinite Ideas*
Robert McKee, *Story: Substance, Structure, Style and the Principles of Screenwriting*
Caroline Myss, *Anatomy of the Spirit: The Seven Stages of Power and Healing*
James Nestor, *Breath: The New Science of a Lost Art*
Mary Oliver, *Devotions: The Selected Poems of Mary Oliver*
George Saunders, *A Swim in the Pond in the Rain*
Twyla Tharp, *The Creative Habit: Learn It and Use It for Life*
Mathew Walker, *Why We Sleep: The New Science of Sleep and Dreams*
David Whyte, *Essentials*
John Yorke, *Into the Woods: How Stories Work and Why We Tell Them*

Dr Andrew Huberman – listen to his podcast about neuroscience to self-regulate emotion
The London Screenwriters' Festival – my favourite, inspirational resource for any writer
Marie Popova, The Marginalian – formerly known as Brain Pickings – fabulous blog that celebrates fully integrating thought and feeling in creativity

ACKNOWLEDGMENTS

FOR MUM & SALLY, NICK & ARCHIE BALDOCK

No book is an island. Each one comes to life with enormous support from family, friends and colleagues. Huge appreciation goes to my agent Sallyanne Sweeney and Writers & Artists editor Alysoun Owen for asking me to write this book. I thrived in a pandemic, bolstered by your kind professionalism. Hats off to my fierce copy-editor Jill Laidlaw and proofreader Lisa Carden; a fearless, heavily pregnant Eden Phillips Harrington, and the publishing teams at Bloomsbury and Writers & Artists who sell, design, typeset, proofread and catch my mistakes. Thank you, Barbara Kennedy, my critique group: Annette, Louise, Alison, Susan, for your eyes on the manuscript. Shout out to Chris Jones, The London Screenwriters' Festival, SCBWI, Swaggers, The Bath Novel Award, Caroline Ambrose, Bath Spa MA-ers, Amanda, Grace, Annie, the Roses, Jenkins, and Sally Reardon, for your ability to scale new heights. My thanks to David Whyte for allowing me to use his wonderful, wise poem 'Start Close In'. Thank you, Caroline Myss, Jean Houston, Dr Andrew Huberman and the late John O'Donohue for knowledge I didn't process.

Above all, I am grateful to four key people: my 96-year-old mother, Maureen Smit, who cheered me on as I wrote this workbook and school friend Sally Thirkettle, whose conversations were my compass and muse for a tandem book that wrote itself – 'A Writer's Soul Journey'. I recommend you find a friend or tribe to share insights, observations and self-knowledge whenever you read or write a book – you laugh more and travel further together. My home champions are Nick and Archie Baldock – thank you darlings for all your love, tech rescues and endless good humour.

Extracts appear on these pages: pp 51–2 'Start Close in' by David Whyte, printed with permission from Many Rivers Press, www.davidwhyte.com © Many Rivers Press, Langley, WA USA; p 62 from *Hamnet* © Maggie O'Farrell 2020; p 65 from *Gods and Warriors* © Michelle Paver 2012; p 96 from *I Capture the Castle* © Dodie Smith 1949.